Praise for *Just Show Up*

In a world of shortcuts, cheap tricks, and life hacks, Drew Dyck's creative and winsome book stands out with solid biblical wisdom. How do we succeed in life, faith, and relationships? Sometimes it's as simple as showing up. Let Drew give you a practical demonstration of the power of faithfulness—and how it can benefit every area of our lives.

LEE STROBEL, bestselling author of *The Case for Christ* and *The Case for Heaven*

Don't be deceived by the simple title of this book. The advice is simple but not simplistic. It's hard to "just show up" when relationships are broken, when church is boring, and when reading your Bible isn't bearing any obvious fruit. And it's easy to sit at home, bingeing your favorite TV show. But the seemingly small acts of just showing up will pay unimaginable dividends in time—love being chief among them.

BETHANY JENKINS, Vice President of Media, Veritas Forum

As I read *Just Show Up*, I kept thinking of all the people I can't wait to share it with. But most of all I grew aware that the message was for me, first. This book made me feel seen, understood, and inspired. It also made me laugh and read sections out loud to my family. *Just Show Up* will change lives. It's already changing mine.

MONICA SWANSON, author of *Raising Amazing* and *Boy Mom*, and host of the *Monica Swanson Podcast*

Have you ever felt like you weren't making an impact? In our world of influencers and social media fame, it can feel like we are constantly falling behind. However, over and over in the Bible, God uses seemingly insignificant people to accomplish great things. In *Just Show Up*, Drew Dyck emphasizes the importance of "just showing up" and being faithful, even in the small things. A highly encouraging read!

JORDAN RAYNOR, bestselling author of *Redeeming Your Time* and *Master of One*

Drew might come across as the guy next door, but in fact, he is a storyteller who disarms you with his "aw shucks" demeanor while dishing out practical, biblical, and life-changing truth. While most Christians may understand the importance of faithfulness, Drew vividly illustrates what that life of faithfulness looks like with both personal stories and biblical examples. If you're longing to make an impact in the kingdom of God but aren't sure how to do it, get this book.

LINA ABUJAMRA, founder of Living With Power ministries and author of *Fractured Faith: Finding Your Way Back to God in an Age of Deconstruction*

Modern Christians often feel the pressure to "change the world" with headline-grabbing acts, but sometimes the most radical thing you can do is to simply be present in the areas where God has called you. *Just Show Up* is a refreshing reminder that real courage shows up in the nitty-gritty of our daily lives and that the boring rhythms of obedience are the substance of a meaningful life. Drew Dyck offers a manifesto for the mundane, a road map for faithfulness, reminding us that the kingdom of God is made up of mostly ordinary people saying yes to God in ways that will never make the evening news.

DANIEL DARLING, director of the Land Center for Cultural Engagement, columnist, and bestselling author of several books, including *The Dignity Revolution*, *The Characters of Christmas*, and *Agents of Grace*

Reading this book is like taking a walk with a good friend who is equal parts encouraging and wise, vulnerably walking with you as a fellow traveler who has traversed the path many times before. This book is an invitation to take a deep breath; it's a smile and a knowing laugh when someone fully describes what you just went through that day. This book is a guide on how to do big things in the very small with consistency and humility leading the way. Drew Dyck is one of my favorite voices. I especially loved how he sets the stage in this book: "That's how things work in God's economy. He provides the feast. You just show up." This is the kind of book you read and just want to thank the author. So, thank you Drew.

PAUL ANGONE, bestselling author of *101 Secrets for Your Twenties* and *Listen to Your Day: The Life-Changing Practice of Paying Attention*

We all want success tomorrow. Or better yet today! But the truth is, success is slow. It's the people who put in the work, day after day, that reach their goals. *Just Show Up* is a powerful reminder of that fact. Using biblical and contemporary stories, Drew demonstrates how showing up for the most important things in your life pays off over time.

JON ACUFF, *New York Times* bestselling author of *Soundtracks: The Surprising Solution to Overthinking*

JUST SHOW

How Small Acts of Faithfulness Change Everything

A GUIDE FOR EXHAUSTED CHRISTIANS

DREW DYCK

MOODY PUBLISHERS
CHICAGO

© 2023 by
DREW DYCK

All rights reserved. No part of this book may be reproduced in any form without permission in writing from the publisher, except in the case of brief quotations embodied in critical articles or reviews.

All Scripture quotations, unless otherwise indicated, are taken from the Holy Bible, New International Version®, NIV®. Copyright ©1973, 1978, 1984, 2011 by Biblica, Inc.™ Used by permission of Zondervan. All rights reserved worldwide. www.zondervan.com The "NIV" and "New International Version" are trademarks registered in the United States Patent and Trademark Office by Biblica, Inc.™

Scripture quotations marked (NLT) are taken from the *Holy Bible*, New Living Translation, copyright ©1996, 2004, 2015 by Tyndale House Foundation. Used by permission of Tyndale House Publishers, Carol Stream, Illinois 60188. All rights reserved.

Scripture quotations marked NASB are taken from the (NASB®) New American Standard Bible®, Copyright © 1960, 1971, 1977, 1995, 2020 by The Lockman Foundation. Used by permission. All rights reserved. lockman.org

Scripture quotations marked NKJV are taken from the New King James Version®. Copyright © 1982 by Thomas Nelson. Used by permission. All rights reserved.

Edited by Connor Sterchi
Interior design: Ragont Design
Cover photo and design: Erik M. Peterson
Author photo: Bethany Villero

Library of Congress Cataloging-in-Publication Data

Names: Dyck, Drew, author.
Title: Just show up : how small acts of faithfulness change everything (a guide for exhausted Christians) / Drew Dyck.
Description: Chicago, IL : Moody Publishers, [2023] | Includes bibliographical references. | Summary: "We tend to think it's the big, bold moments that matter. In reality, it's the steady accumulation of small acts of obedience to God that add up to an impactful life of meaning. Drew Dyck recounts biblical and personal stories of how God rewards the persistent presence of ordinary people"-- Provided by publisher.
Identifiers: LCCN 2023007184 (print) | LCCN 2023007185 (ebook) | ISBN 9780802428585 | ISBN 9780802475244 (ebook)
Subjects: LCSH: Friendship--Religious aspects. | Christian life.
Classification: LCC BV4647.F7 D93 2023 (print) | LCC BV4647.F7 (ebook) | DDC 205/.6762--dc23/eng/20230523
LC record available at https://lccn.loc.gov/2023007184
LC ebook record available at https://lccn.loc.gov/2023007185

Originally delivered by fleets of horse-drawn wagons, the affordable paperbacks from D. L. Moody's publishing house resourced the church and served everyday people. Now, after more than 125 years of publishing and ministry, Moody Publishers' mission remains the same—even if our delivery systems have changed a bit. For more information on other books (and resources) created from a biblical perspective, go to www.moodypublishers.com or write to:

Moody Publishers
820 N. LaSalle Boulevard
Chicago, IL 60610

1 3 5 7 9 10 8 6 4 2

Printed in the United States of America

To my daughter Mary.
I'm so glad you showed up.

Contents

Introduction

My (Only Slightly Sad) Midlife Manifesto

How Hitting My Limits Led to a Freeing Realization

None of the kids were going to sleep. And it had already been a long day.

I'd started work with a series of Zoom meetings at 7 a.m. and didn't close my laptop till dinnertime. My wife, Grace, spent the day homeschooling our two oldest kids while chasing our restless toddler. The toddler had invented an exciting game. She would climb up onto the table where her brother and sister were doing homework, sweep all the pencils and pens onto the ground, and tear up their papers.

"Mom!" our six-year-old howled. "She's doing it again!"

Now we were running through the nighttime routine. Feeding, bathing, dressing, brushing, coaxing, pleading, screaming (them), crying (me).

It was a marathon.

When it was finally time for bed, we divided to conquer. Grace took the toddler; I took the big kids. I told them a story, said a quick prayer, and kissed them good night.

"Okay, guys. Time to sleep."

Yeah, right. Thirty minutes later I could hear them squealing and jumping around. I went in and discovered that they were diving into a pile of pillows in the middle of the room. Had I been less grumpy, I might have noticed how cute they were. But I was in no mood. "GO TO SLEEP!" I thundered. Mary's lip started to tremble. Then sobs. I ordered her brother back to the top bunk and I lay down beside her. Finally, they both nodded off.

Meanwhile, our two-year-old angel was acting more like a demon, screaming in her crib. Grace tried to rock her, but she would escape from her lap, run around the room, then rip off her diaper and hand it to Grace like a present.

When Grace finally emerged, shutting the door quietly behind her, she exhaled slowly. "These days are loooong."

It was after 10 p.m. We'd planned to watch some TV but knew the kids would be up at the crack of dawn. "Maybe we should just go to bed," I said.

As we lay in bed, Grace smiled grimly. "Tough day."

"Is life this hard for everyone?" I wondered aloud.

"I don't know," she said. "But we're doing it. And we'll do it again tomorrow."

FLASHBACK

In the early days of our marriage, life looked quite different. Shortly after our wedding we moved from Portland, Oregon, to

Pasadena, California, where I enrolled in seminary. I'd briefly considered going to law school but settled on seminary simply because, well, I wanted to study theology. I didn't want to be a pastor (that's what my dad did) or a professor (that was too much school). I wanted to write, to communicate God's truth. But I didn't know anyone who made a living doing that. The truth is I had no clear vocational objectives. But somehow it made sense to take out a bunch of student loans and move a thousand miles away to study about God.

We sold everything that wouldn't fit into our Volkswagen Beetle and struck out for California. After living in the gray and rainy Northwest, driving into Pasadena felt like rolling into heaven. The seminary campus was idyllic, with a commons area that featured sculptures, a prayer garden, and pathways lined with palm trees. The seminary café served sandwiches named after famous theologians. On any given day you could spot Grace and me sitting cross-legged with other seminarians on the grass eating a Dietrich Bonhoeffer or a Karl Barth (they were delicious) while discussing the New Perspective on Paul or the proper relationship between art and the church. Grace, who is a painter, worked at a center that hosted lectures on art and theology. At night we attended lectures from visiting scholars, went to art galleries, or watched plays. We swam in a world of ideas.

When we talked about the future, we had big, if amorphous, plans.

"I don't want the average life. Who cares about the American Dream?" I'd say to Grace.

She was right there with me. "Let's do something . . . different."

It wasn't about being cool or original. Well, maybe a little. But most of all, we wanted to do something big for God. We were moved by the plight of the poor and the great needs of the world. We were passionate about sharing our faith. And we made attempts to live out our values. We'd go to soup kitchens to serve meals or head down to a mission in LA's Skid Row for a karaoke night with the homeless. At one point, we got tired of piling up knowledge about God in our heads and ventured to the main strip in Pasadena, Colorado Boulevard, to hand out copies of the gospel of John and strike up spiritual conversations with strangers.

Our small attempts to change the world didn't result in much change, but we weren't discouraged. It was a foretaste of what we assumed would be an exciting and countercultural life together. Maybe it would involve going overseas or starting a nonprofit. We realized it would mean forgoing or delaying some of the milestones of a typically "successful" life, but we didn't mind. Other people can chase the white picket fence and have 2.5 children. We were going to do something radical.

SHOWING UP

It's a little embarrassing even writing those words now. Our life is great, but it has turned out differently than what we envisioned as we ate theological sandwiches beneath the palm trees in Pasadena. Today I paid the mortgage, washed our minivan, and took the family out for dinner. At Olive Garden. We don't have 2.5 children. We have three. We don't have a white picket fence, but now that I mention it, I wonder how much one would cost.

Life comes at you fast.

Maybe you can relate. You started your journey into adulthood with a bright burst of idealism—and then slammed into reality. You were going to do something dramatic and different only to find it's hard just to make it. As the years rolled on, your life got busier, tougher. One day you woke up with more responsibilities and less free time. Now you juggle a host of competing priorities: career, family, health, friends, church. It feels like if someone adds one more thing to your to-do list, you might crumble. At the same time, those dreams you had early on are still there, nagging faintly at the back of your mind. Or receding out on the horizon as you move toward them in slow motion.

If that's you, you're holding the right book. I wrote this book for you, and honestly, for myself too.

I haven't figured it all out, but I've discovered some things along the way.

One is that we're not called to change the world. God doesn't require us to do something big and dramatic to fulfill His call on our lives. My younger self would be disappointed to hear that. But now it's a relief. Saving the world sounds exhausting and I just don't have the energy these days. Instead, God calls us to small acts of ordinary faithfulness. This kind of success doesn't come in spite of life's responsibilities and challenges, but in the midst of them. Even because of them. It might not change the world, but it does change us and the people around us.

This hit home for me recently when Grace asked me to name the people I most admired. My list didn't contain one person who was powerful or famous. In fact, most weren't especially talented or charismatic. So why did I admire them? Because they were faithful. One was a small church pastor who kept teaching and leading despite a debilitating illness. Another started a soup kitchen. And she kept feeding the homeless, even after losing her husband.

These people didn't win my respect because they did something daring and dramatic. It was because they persevered. They kept getting up and coming back and pushing ahead. They continued serving and loving and praying and believing. They obeyed God's call to run the race, even when the best they could do was place one wobbly leg in front of another.

They just showed up. That has become a mantra for me. A prayer. It might sound a little silly, but I repeat it to myself when I'm disappointed or discouraged.

Just show up.

In the pages ahead, you'll see the powerful truth contained in this simple, three-word phrase. I'm going to show you examples from Scripture of how God used people who showed up. And I'm going to tell contemporary stories of how He's still doing that today. We're going to look at the incredible things that happen through the power of simply being a persistent presence. I want to challenge you to show up in your life for the people around you. We're going to explore what it looks like to show up for your family, for your work, for your community, and for your friends. Most importantly, I'm going to ask you to show up for God. And I want to inspire you to keep showing up, even when you're weary or discouraged or uncertain.

A CRUCIAL COMMITMENT

Showing up is a simple commitment. But it's not a trivial one. As I started researching for this book, I got excited thinking about how my life would change if I put this principle into action. How would my marriage transform if I consistently showed up for my wife, putting her needs above my own? What would happen if I showed up for our kids? Not just physically, but if I put down my phone more often and gave them my full attention? How would things change if I tackled my work with passion and intentionality instead of sleepwalking through my daily to-do list? How would my life change if I showed up to commune with God every day and spent time in His Word?

What got me even more excited was thinking about the effect it would have if thousands of others began doing the same. What impact would it have on families? How would our communities change if neighbors showed up for each other? What would happen if we refused to walk past needs hoping someone else would do something about them? What if we started showing up for people who were lonely, desperate, and hurting? It would mean fewer people slipping through the cracks. More people feeling welcomed and loved. There would be less depression and alienation. Fewer suicides and incidents of violence. No abandoned children. No neglected friends. Destructive generational patterns would be interrupted. Whole communities would begin to heal.

Does that get you excited too? If it feels too abstract to imagine the large-scale impact, think smaller. How would showing up affect you? What difference would it make for your friends and family? For your relationship with God? For the work God has called you to do? In the pages ahead, I hope you catch a vision for how adopting this simple commitment could transform your life and bless the people around you.

In the gospel of Luke, Jesus tells a story about a man who prepares a great feast. Then he sends out his servant to invite his friends to the banquet. But they all decline his invitation. They make excuses. One says he's just bought a piece of land and needs to tend to it. Another sends his regrets, saying he recently purchased some livestock. A third says he can't come because he just got married.

The man is furious. He instructs his servant to go out and invite anyone who wants to come to the feast. "Go out to the roads and country lanes and compel them to come in, so that my house will be full," he says (Luke 14:23).

Jesus uses the story to describe what the kingdom of God is like. Whole books have been written about this powerful parable, but one thing jumps out at me. The people who end up eating at the great feast only have one thing in common: they showed up. They weren't even supposed to be there. None of them were on the guest list. They were strangers, random people off the street. Some of them probably homeless. But they did something the others were unwilling to do. When they got the call, they came.

That's how things work in God's economy. He provides the feast. You just show up.

Those invited guests had a lot of excuses not to show up. Good excuses. I'll bet you have excuses too. You're tired. Too busy. You don't have the right credentials. You don't feel prepared. You have too much going on. But there are people who need you. People who won't make it without you. Most importantly, God is calling you. He's prepared a feast. And the table is ready.

Chapter One

Join the Plodders

You Don't Have to Move Fast. You Just Have to Keep Moving.

My dad struggled in school. So much so that his academic woes became part of our family lore. Thankfully, he had a sense of humor about it.

"My sixth grade teacher liked me so much," he'd say, "that she decided to keep me for an extra year!"

To be fair, my dad's early life wasn't exactly easy. For years, his eleven-member Mennonite family lived in a one-bedroom farmhouse on the Canadian prairies. It had no electricity, no running water. The children took a bath once a week . . . using the same bathwater. The biggest kid would go first, then the second biggest, right down to the smallest child. As the youngest in my family, hearing that story always made my skin crawl—and thank God for indoor plumbing.

They spoke low German at home, which meant when my dad started school, he had to learn a new language: English. After rising early to do farm chores, he walked to school (uphill both ways, of course) with a temporary limp he'd gotten from contracting polio as a toddler. Exhausted, he'd often drift off during class.

He eked through elementary school, passing on probation until he encountered that teacher who kept him for an extra year. In high school he found refuge in basketball and track, but his academic struggles continued. His lackluster performance in the classroom wasn't a concern, however. His parents assumed he would follow his father into carpentry or join his brother in the sheet metal business, neither of which would require him to attend college. But as a teenager, he felt called to the ministry. And after high school he enrolled in Bible college.

Unfortunately, his academic challenges followed him. He picked up Cs and Ds, despite studying for hours each night. After the first year, he received a letter from the administration department of the college. It advised him not to return.

He was devastated. "I fell on my bed and sobbed," he recalls. "I didn't know what to do." His parents had supported his decision to pursue his calling but even they started to waver. On a trip home, his dad suggested that maybe it was time for him to come home and work carpentry instead. But my dad couldn't shake the feeling that he was called to ministry. His denomination required that he get a degree from Bible school to get ordained. He had to graduate.

The next fall he walked onto campus determined to turn things around. Yet he still struggled to make good grades. That summer he experienced a strong sense of déjà vu when he found himself opening another letter from the college, saying the same thing. *Don't come back.*

Finally, in the last year, his grades improved. The change was in part thanks to the young American student that he'd married that summer (hi, Mom!). She took charge of his schedule, breaking each assignment into manageable parts and assigning it to a specific week on the calendar. She also taught him to study smart. "He was trying to memorize everything," she recalled. "But it helped him to focus on learning what was going to be on the tests."

He was also spurred along by a professor who believed in him. "Art, you're going to be a wonderful pastor because you love people so much," the professor told him. Slowly things turned around. He started doing better on tests. Essays came back with less red ink and more positive comments. He finished the year with an A- average, which lifted his cumulative GPA above the required 2.0.

He graduated.

As he walked down the aisle to receive his diploma, one of his professors shook his hand and confessed, "I honestly didn't think you'd make it."

A POWERFUL PRINCIPLE

I heard that story many times growing up. To be honest, it was always hard to square with the man my dad had become: a powerful preacher with an encyclopedic knowledge of the Bible. One thing that was easy to see is that the prediction of that encouraging professor had come true. My dad was a wonderful pastor. He loved people, and they loved him. Every church he led—from the tiny rural congregation to a large, prestigious church in the city—flourished. The guy who barely made it through Bible school ended up planting two churches, leading four, and starting a soup kitchen that feeds thousands of people to this day. Along the way, he prayed with hundreds of people to accept Jesus. There are many people who trace the beginning of their spiritual journey to the influence of my dad. I'm one of them.

When I reflect on my dad's story, I'm grateful that he didn't give up on his calling. I think of all the people who wouldn't have heard about Jesus, wouldn't have been counseled, visited, or encouraged. I think of the thousands who wouldn't have been fed spiritually (and physically) had he not become a pastor. The world would have been worse off.

Showing up means being willing to take that first scary step toward what you feel God is calling you to do. And then do it again.

When I ask my dad how he overcame the barriers that would have scared most people away, he doesn't really have an answer. There was no dramatic moment in his story, no brilliant strategy to turn things around. He just came back for classes every fall.

He kept showing up.

Which brings me back to the core concept of this book. What does it mean to show up? Often it requires that you are physically present, like my dad turning up for class. But it's bigger than that. It's about moving through your life with a commitment to attend to the most important things. And it requires action. It means being willing to take that first scary step toward what you feel God is calling you to do. And then do it again.

As I thought about people who embody this approach to life, I realized they share at least two characteristics. They have deep faith. And they plod.

DEEP FAITH

The most essential factor to showing up? Deep faith.

Hebrews 11 is one of my favorite passages in all of Scripture. It's often called the "hall of faith," and it's not hard to see why. The chapter lists the exploits of biblical characters like Abel, Abraham, Noah, Moses, Joseph, and Rahab. Each is lauded for obeying God in the face of great difficulty. Abraham strikes out from his home when God calls him, "even though he did not know where he was going" (Heb. 11:8). Noah builds an entire ark before a drop of rain falls. Moses leaves the luxury of Pharaoh's palace to side with the enslaved Hebrews, choosing "to be mistreated along with the people of God rather than to enjoy the pleasures of sin for a short time" (Heb. 11:25).

How did they take these extraordinary actions? "By faith." The words "by faith" appear twenty-one times in the passage. How do we know these Bible heroes acted by faith? Because many times they never saw the rewards for their righteous behavior. "All these people were still living by faith when they died. They did not receive the things promised; they only saw them and welcomed them from a distance," the writer of Hebrews explains (Heb. 11:13). Yet they pressed on, convinced that God saw their obedience and would reward them. If not in this life, then in the one to come (Heb. 11:16).

We call these people "heroes," but they were far from perfect. Dig into their stories. They were every bit as fallible as us. But they had an abiding faith in God. And it propelled them forward in the face of unimaginable adversity. Ultimately it wasn't their talents or toughness that made them prevail. They did it "by faith."

In the coming chapters we're going to look at what it means to show up in the most important areas of your life: for your family and friends, for your community, and for yourself. But I want to state this truth upfront: *none of it works without faith.*

Without faith, it's easy to give up. If your only confidence is in your own strength and abilities, you'll throw in the towel the moment life throws a few punches at you. You might show up when things are good—when the weather is pleasant, and the sun is shining. But as soon as dark clouds appear and the winds of life start howling, you'll pack it in.

But when you're grounded in the unshakable promises of God, you can walk through the storm. You know that even if no one else sees what you're doing, God does. You endure hardship in the present because you believe God will reward you in the future. You keep walking because you know that, even when you stumble, God has promised to catch you.

My dad's persistence in pursuing his calling wasn't rooted in a belief in his abilities. It was anchored in confidence in the God who was calling him. He knew he didn't have the academic chops to make it through college, but he believed God was calling him to be a pastor, so he kept pushing ahead, kept showing up.

Living by faith isn't easy (we'll talk about that more in a coming chapter). But it frees you from the tyranny of your feelings and changing circumstances. It gives you a North Star to help guide you in darkness. You don't have to rely on in-the-moment calculations on whether doing the right thing will pay off; you know it will. You don't "grow weary of doing good" because you know that "at the proper time [you] will reap a harvest if [you] do not give up" (Gal. 6:9).

So, you stay on the path, sometimes running, sometimes crawling, but always moving forward—in faith.

"I CAN PLOD"

Another key to showing up? Plodding.

William Carey, the "father of modern missions," accomplished more in one lifetime than most people could in ten. He helped translate the Bible into forty-four languages, ran an orphanage, founded a college, started a horticultural society, and worked tirelessly to end cruel practices in India, such as female infanticide. But according to Carey, the secret to his prodigious accomplishments could be boiled down to one rather dull skill.

"I can plod," Carey wrote.

Plodding is a boring word. Even saying it is dull. And the definition isn't much better. "Slow, continuous, and not exciting," is how the Cambridge dictionary puts it.[1] "To move, progress, or develop at a slow but constant and deliberate pace," another dictionary explains.[2]

Plodding is slow, laborious. It doesn't sound very sexy. But here's the key to plodding's power: it's *continuous* and *constant*. Plodders don't move fast—but they keep moving.

Carey personified this. We marvel at what he achieved. But if you could zoom in on any given day of Carey's life, it probably wouldn't look that exciting. You might see him sitting in a study with ink-stained hands, translating the Bible, word by word, into Sanskrit. Or catch a glimpse of him peeling potatoes for the hungry children at his orphanage. You might spot him setting up chairs for the open-air services he held to preach, even though it would be more than six years before he saw one convert. You'd see a plodder.

Carey did remarkable things, but not because he had remarkable talent. It was because, as he said, he could plod.

"I can persevere in any definite pursuit," he wrote. "To this I owe everything."[3]

In my early twenties I tried to be a financial adviser. To motivate myself I spent hours dreaming about everything I planned to accomplish. I even made a "dream board" filled with all the fun things I was going to purchase once I experienced success. As I recall, it had a picture of a fancy car and a shot of a beach to represent the Hawaiian vacation I was going to take. I loved dreaming! You know what I didn't like? Getting on the phone and calling prospective clients. That was hard and scary. It was far more fun to dream. It's no surprise that my stint as a financial adviser lasted less than two years.

In contrast, I recently read about a young man working in the same industry who took a different approach. Trent Dyrsmid was only twenty-three years old when he was hired as a stockbroker, but he experienced success quickly. He attributed his success to an odd habit. Each day he would put two jars on his desk. One was empty, the other had 120 paper clips in it. Every time he made a sales call, he would transfer one paper clip to the empty jar—and wouldn't stop until he transferred all 120 paper clips. Within no time, Dyrsmid was bringing $5 million dollars into the firm.[4]

Plodding isn't glamorous. But all those little steps add up. And God uses them in amazing ways.

Why did Trent succeed where I failed? Well, dreaming is fun. More fun than making calls and moving paper clips. But doing hard, boring work is what brings results. Plodding means being more of a paper clip person and less of a "dream board" one. And it applies to more than your career. It affects every area of life.

What is a plodder? Just someone who shows up. Over and over again. Plodding isn't glamorous. But all those little steps add up. And God uses them in amazing ways.

My dad was a plodder. I always used to see the academic challenges he faced early in life as an impediment to his calling. Now I believe they fueled it. Those challenges steeled his resolve and shaped his unique approach to ministry.

When he took his first church, he made a goal of visiting every house of the small town and surrounding area. And that's exactly what he did. He'd knock on doors and ask people if they needed prayer. Some turned him away, but most were receptive. He was invited into nice houses and served fresh apple pie. Or waved into filthy dwellings overrun with cats. But he got to pray with strangers. Listen to their problems. Help with household chores. Tell them about Jesus.

One time, he knocked on the door of a farmhouse, but no one was home. As he walked back to his 1969 station wagon, he spotted smoke drifting up from behind the house. The fence had caught fire and the flames were moving toward the barn. He sprinted toward the fence and used the water from a feeding trough to douse the flames. When the farmer learned about what he'd done, a friendship was born. The farmer and his wife came to church and decided to follow Jesus. I reflected on that story recently when I had lunch with the son of those farmers, now a missionary pilot in Africa.

My dad's visitation strategy paid off, and the church swelled to twice its former size. More and more people in that small farming community started following Jesus, even some of the ones who had originally turned my dad away at the door.

If my dad's life had been easy, I doubt he would have knocked on every door in town. If school had been a breeze, he might not have pushed past his natural shyness to visit suspicious strangers. But he was used to doing hard things. Those early obstacles strengthened him and taught him not to give up.

The secret to plodding is patience. "I'm struck by how often the life of faith is described as a 'walk,'" writes pastor Luke Simmons. "It's steady plodding, one step at a time. And sometimes the win for the day is just that you kept walking."[5] It's a point echoed by my friend Daniel Darling. In writing about the story of Noah, he observed, "We look at the big boat, but the way Noah trusted God was by picking up his hammer every morning and hammering in another nail."[6]

When you're a plodder, you likely won't see dramatic breakthroughs every day. You must be okay with incremental progress, with small and sporadic victories. You must make peace with frustrations and setbacks and delays. We're often wrong about obstacles. They're blessings, not burdens. When you're committed to plodding, you look back on them and see how they ended up helping you along.

Earlier I mentioned how William Carey translated the Bible into forty-four languages. The translations were almost lost to history when the building where they were stored burned to the ground. But Carey went right back to work, painstakingly reproducing each translation. Ultimately, he concluded that "out of catastrophe God had brought permanent enrichment."[7]

My colleague Catherine Parks writes biographies about great Christians of the past. But after immersing herself in scores of these stories, she told me that she's struck by how ordinary these people were. "We think of them as giants, these spiritual superheroes. But they were just doing the next thing in front of them. They were scared, just like we are. But they were faithful."

SEE THE WORK BEGIN

La Sagrada Família in Barcelona is one of the most spectacular buildings on earth. Designed by nineteenth-century architect Antoni Gaudí, it attracts more than five million tourists each year. La Sagrada Família looks completely different from other European churches. Gaudí put a modern twist on Gothic architecture to create a structure with an intricate style and unique design. The lines of the Spanish basilica are smooth and twisting, which reflects Gaudí's commitment to natural design. As the architect once observed, "There are no straight lines or sharp corners in nature."[8]

Sadly, I haven't visited La Sagrada Família. My brother traveled to the famous church recently and texted me pictures. I almost couldn't believe they were real. Inside, treelike pillars stretch up to the church's kaleidoscopic ceiling where brilliant colors pour through stained-glass windows. Outside, massive, ornate spires stretch more than five hundred feet into the sky. The decorative exterior makes the whole structure look a little spooky, like a massive, melting sandcastle. Art critic Rainer Zerbst said "it is probably impossible to find a church building anything like it in the entire history of art."[9]

I was even more intrigued by the structure when I read about its history. Gaudí spent the last forty-three years of his life working on the church. A dedicated Christian, he saw the project as his life's mission and filled the house of worship with façades depicting biblical scenes. As construction of the church dragged on, many became impatient. Yet Gaudí was unwilling to rush his magnum opus. When asked why the church was taking so long to complete, Gaudí responded, "My client is not in a hurry."[10]

Construction on La Sagrada Família started in 1882. It is still being built, more than 140 years later. But Gaudí's grand vision impacts millions, beautifully bearing witness to the glory of the God he served.

You might be thinking that you're no Gaudí. Or William Carey. Don't worry. Neither am I. But there's no telling what God can do through humble servants who keep showing up, who aren't too proud to plod. When you first start plodding, not much happens. The early results are modest, but that's okay. Don't get discouraged. Remember, like Gaudí, you are working for an audience of One. And He is not in a hurry.

In the book of Zechariah, God relays a message through His prophet: "Do not despise these small beginnings, for the LORD rejoices to see the work begin" (Zech. 4:10 NLT). The beginnings in question referred to the foundation of the unfinished temple that God assured Zechariah would be rebuilt.

I believe the principle applies to our lives as well. God doesn't sit back with folded arms, waiting for us to reach perfection. He "rejoices to see the work begin." And He doesn't demand it happen all at once. He only asks you to take the next step.

REFLECT

Does the idea of plodding appeal to you? What obstacles prevent you from plodding?

What does "walking by faith" mean to you? How might your life change if you rooted your confidence in God's abilities and not your own?

This chapter defined showing up as "being willing to take that first scary step toward what you feel God is calling you to do." Is there something you feel God is calling you to do that you've been reluctant to pursue? If so, what's the "first scary step" you need to take?

Chapter Two

Show Up In Person

Because People Need Your Presence More than Your Words

Chon Armsbury is the luckiest guy I know.

Or at least, he seems to be. He has won not one, not two, but *three* fully paid trips to Hawaii.

The truth is my friend's winning streak is only partially due to luck. He also did some strategic maneuvering. When he first saw his 24-hour fitness gym advertising a raffle for a Hawaiian vacation, he resolved to do everything he could do to increase his chances of winning. He learned you could fill out an entry form each time you worked out—and he did.

"I worked out every day just to enter the contest," he told me. "Sometimes I worked out twice a day, so I could fill out an extra one."

There was a catch, however, which ended up working in his favor. To win the prize, you had to be physically present for the drawing. Thousands had likely entered. But when the day arrived, only about a hundred people came out. Chon knew he had decent odds. He'd probably stuffed more entries into the raffle box than anyone else. But when they called his name, he still couldn't believe it.

"I jumped around like Michael Jordan after hitting a game-winner," he recalls.

After taking his wife, Melanie, on a lovely trip to Hawaii, he started wondering if he could win again.

The next year he dutifully filled out an entry form after each workout. When the day of the raffle came again, he found himself waiting for the drawing, this time with even fewer people. They announced they would also be giving away some water bottles. When they called Chon's name, that's what he thought he had won—a water bottle. He stepped forward glumly to accept his plastic prize.

"Can I still win the trip to Hawaii?" he asked. "No, you don't understand," they told him. "You won the trip!"

More Jordan jumping.

Now he was hooked, but the next year that terrible law of averages kicked in and the prize went to someone else. For Year Four, he was working out at a different location, but they were running the same contest. When the day of the drawing came, they announced the winner—but the person wasn't present. They called out another, but no one responded. In fact, they called eight winners before drawing the name of someone who was present. And, you guessed it, that person was Chon.

Free Hawaii trip #3!

What's Chon's secret to winning? Simple. "You gotta be there."

"People put in an entry form, but they don't think they're going to win," he said. "So, they just don't come."

You can probably see why I'm telling you about Chon's winning streak. It's a fun little story that illustrates the principle at the heart of this book. Showing up is everything. In chapter 1, I wrote that showing up isn't just about being physically present. There are many ways we can show up for others. But I'm adding a crucial qualifier to that statement.

There's nothing better than being physically present.

TOGETHER, BUT ALONE

It's never been easier to avoid people. Technology has enabled us to do almost everything all by ourselves. If I want some entertainment, there's no need to leave my house. I just stream a movie. Need to do some shopping? Malls are so 2003. I just go to Amazon.com and get same-day delivery. I work from home, so I don't have to go into an office. Almost all my meetings are on Zoom. If I find even virtual meetings too personal, I can always shut off my camera and interact with my colleagues as a disembodied voice. Hungry? I tap an app and thirty minutes later food appears at my door (I really need to do this less; it's expensive . . . and fattening). If I have to leave my house, I carry a little glowing, rectangular device in my pocket that helps me escape into my own virtual world, even when surrounded by people.

Instead of creating a global village, it's broken us into millions of little lonely islands.

Ah, paradise, right? Not quite. I've found that when I let myself slip into a world buffered by technologies, I begin feeling numb. Less human. I'll bet you can relate. The new technologies that were supposed to connect the world and bring us all closer together have, in some ways, done the opposite. Instead of creating a global village, it's broken us into millions of little lonely islands.

Try a little thought experiment with me. Imagine aliens visit our planet. Not angry, invading aliens. Curious, academic ones who just want to observe our behavior. If their spaceship touched down in North America, and they peered through our windows, what would they see?

They might be surprised to learn that the most intelligent creatures on the planet spend, on average, nearly twenty-two hours a week watching flickering pixels move across large screens[1]—and another twenty-eight hours staring at smaller screens they hold in their hands.[2] They'd likely conclude that whatever was on those screens must be incredibly exciting.

But their confusion would grow when they realized the truth—that often what was on those screens wasn't all that different from the real world. They'd see us watching shows of other people talking to each other—while we ignore the people around us. They'd see us watching video clips of nature scenes—while ignoring the natural world. They'd see people forgoing romantic relationships with living, breathing partners to lust over two-dimensional images of strangers online.

You'd have to excuse our alien observers for being confused. "Species seems intent on ignoring the real people and pleasures in front of them," they'd record in their extraterrestrial log. "Instead, they spend their days absorbed in a poor facsimile of their external surroundings."

I felt like a confused alien recently when I noticed a group of young people at a restaurant, all on their phones. I wondered if, at some point, they would lower their digital devices and engage each other in conversation. They didn't. Not once. Finally, one of them raised his head and asked, "Everyone done?" and they walked out of the restaurant.

For someone like me, who grew up before the internet, it was a surreal sight. I must have watched them for at least twenty minutes, connected to the internet, but disconnected from each other. Together, but alone.

NARROW, BUT DEEP

During the pandemic, we got a glimpse of what happens when humans are robbed of physical contact. In response to governmental restrictions, many spent months with little or no contact with people outside their homes. Most still had access to phones and the internet. But it wasn't enough. Not nearly. Rates of loneliness, anxiety, and depression shot through the roof.[3]

Virtual connection isn't all bad. But these tools can never replace in-person interactions. If you're in a long-distance relationship, FaceTime is a godsend. But as grateful as you are to have a way to connect, who wants to do that forever? Eventually you want to be together. I've met a lot of people on Twitter and Facebook. But the connections I have been most grateful for are the ones that hopped the digital divide and led to meeting up in real life.

At their best, online connections should facilitate physical gatherings and in-person friendships. Social media is a great tool to communicate ideas and make friends. You can impact greater numbers of people on these platforms. But ultimately, I've found that while your reach through social media may be broad, the impact that you have on people is shallow. In-person relationships, on the other hand, are the opposite. You can only be present with a small number of people, but the impact you have on them is more profound. It's narrow, but deep.

SHOW UP LIKE JESUS

Being physically present is a richer experience. It's healthy and humanizing. But there's a more compelling reason to show up in person. And it's simply this: that's what Jesus did.

We Christians hold to the bizarre and beautiful belief that the God of the universe became a human in the person of Jesus of Nazareth. The disciple John put it this way: "The Word became flesh and made his dwelling among us" (John 1:14). I appreciate the colloquial spin *The Message* puts on this passage: "The Word became flesh and blood, and moved into the neighborhood." I like that because it emphasizes the physical nature of what happened. God truly took on flesh and moved into our midst. Why was it necessary that Jesus come to earth physically? Well, the big reason is that Jesus came to die for our sins. A phantom messiah couldn't do that. We needed a flesh-and-blood Savior.

Being human meant He could identify with our pain and struggles as well. The book of Hebrews says of Jesus, "We do not have a high priest who is unable to empathize with our weaknesses, but we have one who has been tempted in every way, just as we are—yet he did not sin" (Heb. 4:15).

He also came to earth to show us *how* to love each other. And physical presence was central to that mission. Jesus didn't isolate Himself like many spiritual teachers of His time. He dove into the mess of humanity, touching diseased skin and disfigured limbs. He let children sit on His lap and prostitutes anoint His feet. Even when He taught, He often did so with people literally pressing against Him.

We endlessly debate what Jesus would say or do if He was walking the earth today. But there's one thing no honest reader of the Bible can doubt. He would be with people. He would touch people who were desperate and hurting and lonely. And that's exactly what His followers should be doing too.

I must confess I'm not good at this. Right now, I'm writing these words in a coffee shop. A few minutes ago, a homeless man walked in and sat near me. Occasionally, an unpleasant odor wafts over from his table. He's not bothering anyone, but I'm a wimp about bad smells. Now I'm wondering how long I need to sit here before I can leave without hurting his feelings. Yes, I'm wondering this as I'm writing about how Jesus embraced messy, hurting, and (I'm sure) smelly people.

We're never more like Jesus than when we show up in person.

I remember seeing a cartoon where two men are talking. One turns to the other and says, "I love people . . . theoretically." Too often, that's me. I understand all too well the importance of actively loving people, of being with them. But it's easy for me to leave the hands-on stuff to others. I fight the instinct to rope myself off from the muddy stream of humanity and communicate, if at all, from a safe distance. Give me fresh coffee, strong Wi-Fi, and my cozy little family. I'm good.

But that's not the way of Jesus. Following Him means embracing the way He related to others. It requires choosing incarnation over disembodiment. It means being present, even when it's uncomfortable and costly. We're never more like Jesus than when we show up in person.

THE POWER OF PRESENCE

Thankfully I've encountered people who model what it looks like to do this. I think of my son's fourth-grade teacher, Mrs. Heinz. The first time I met her, I didn't know what to think. Her enthusiasm for her students seemed over-the-top. "For me, this isn't just a job," she said, fighting back tears. "It's a calling." I'd soon learn she was serious. Our son was in a basketball league, and she asked if she could attend a game. There are few things more tedious than watching elementary students play basketball (trust me). The games have more turnovers than points. But she wanted to be there for him—and she came.

She also sat in the bleachers for the games of another boy in her class. He wasn't an easy kid to be around. His daily outbursts disrupted the entire class. But Mrs. Heinz started attending his games on the weekends and things began to change. My son told me about how the boy's behavior slowly improved. By the end of the year, he was thriving. I guess when you see that someone cares enough to show up for you, you'll do just about anything to please them. That's the power of presence.

My friend Darryl Forbes pastors a church in Florida. Recently he shared a story about the oldest member of his church. He felt God was nudging him to go visit her in the nursing home—and he went. "She was happier than I'd ever seen her," Darryl wrote. "We talked, sang, and prayed. I had no idea it would be our last visit." She died the next day. "She was one of the original members of the church I pastor," he wrote. "She used to sit on a pillow for comfort. For the last two years we left it where she usually sat. Today I couldn't stop looking at it while I preached. . . . Her battle is won."[4]

I have no doubt that God prompted Darryl to visit her that day. And I'm glad he listened. Without showing up in person, that elderly saint would not have received the loving send-off she so richly deserved. And Darryl would have missed out on providing it for her.

These stories inspire me. They make me want to go the extra mile when I see needs arise. But I don't just know the power of presence secondhand. I've benefited from people showing up for me. I have an anxiety disorder (which I write about more in a later chapter). In the weeks before last Christmas I found myself at a particularly low point. I was struggling to sleep and spent days pacing around my house. My brother Darren heard about what I was going through and one night he sent me a text: "I'm picking you up in thirty minutes."

When I got in his car, he told me about his plan. He wanted to buy winter coats and hand them out to the homeless in downtown Portland. So we went to Costco, and each carried a pile of coats to the checkout. We tucked a twenty-dollar bill into each pocket and spent the night handing them out to grateful men and women shivering on the streets.

But I had a feeling our little mission was more about helping me. And it was exactly what I needed. I had to get out of the house. I needed to stop thinking about my problems. Spending the night helping others was the best thing for my mental health. But I would never have done it if my brother had not shown up that night.

I think most of us want to help when we see others in need. But we stress out over exactly how to help. We worry we won't have the right thing to say. It helps to remember that your presence is usually enough.

Remember Chon, the guy I told you about at the beginning of this chapter who won all the trips to Hawaii? He's seen the principle of physical presence apply to more than just winning raffles. He works for a nonprofit organization called Faithful Friends. They pair adult mentors with at-risk youth. He uses his showing-up philosophy when coaching prospective mentors. "I tell them, 'Don't overthink this, don't overcomplicate. Ninety percent of the value you provide for this child is just showing up. Just being present.'"

That's true for kids and for adults. Social scientist Adam Grant says that when someone is hurting, presence matters more than words.

> In hard times, people don't want to be told to look on the bright side. They want to know you're on their side. Even if you can't help them feel better, you can always help them feel seen. The best way to support others is not to cheer them up. It's to show up.[5]

If you doubt that, just think back to the hardest times in your life. You may remember a thing or two someone said to you. Or you may recall nothing that was said. But I'll bet you remember one thing with perfect clarity—who was there.

A while back, I read a touching story about Ludwig van Beethoven. Because he was deaf, the German composer found social interactions awkward. But when he heard that a friend had lost his son, Beethoven hurried to the man's house. Once inside, he offered no words of comfort, but there was a piano in the room. Beethoven sat down and for half an hour he poured out his grief through his music—and then he left. The friend later remarked that no other visit had been as meaningful.[6]

I love that story. But the scary thing is that Beethoven could have stayed home. He had every reason to. He wasn't good with words. There were other, more eloquent people to comfort the bereaved man. But he showed up and offered what he could. And it was more than enough.

That's true for you too. There are people who need your help. People who are hurting. And if you come alongside them, it will mean the world. You'll find ways to encourage and comfort them. God always puts a piano in the room. Just show up and play it with all your heart!

REFLECT

Why is being physically present so important? What dangers are there in connecting mostly through our devices?

This chapter describes several people who exemplify what it means to show up. Are there people you know who do the same?

Think back to a difficult time in your life. Who showed up for you? How can you show up for others in a similar way?

Chapter Three

Find God's Will with Your Feet

Even When You're "Old"

Kids are cute, but they can be mean.

Years ago, I was standing in a church foyer when a frazzled mother handed me her child so she could wrangle her other kids. It was before I had children, so I held the tyke awkwardly, a good distance from my chest. This turned out to be a mistake because it gave the little girl enough room to study my face and announce her findings.

"Big nose!" she shouted.

I passed her back to her mother.

On another occasion, two boys from our church asked me what I did for a living.

"I'm an author and editor," I responded cheerfully, unaware I was about to be humbled.

"That's too bad," one of them said. "I bet you wish you did something cool, like being a cop or a firefighter."

I was happy with my job—until that moment. Suddenly I realized my bookish career choice ranked rather low on the list of cool jobs in the ten-year-old-male demographic. It was a fact affirmed on Father's Day, when I threw my arms around my own children and told them, "My favorite job is being your dad."

"Of course it is," my son replied. "Your other job is just staring at a computer."

Occasionally, I grow tired of getting absolutely owned by kids and I try to turn the tables. Like recently when I asked my daughter's friends a question.

"What do you want to be when you grow up?"

One wanted to be a princess. The other had plans to become a nurse, like her mother.

That's when I flipped the script.

"What do you think *I* should be when *I* grow up?"

Their foreheads wrinkled. They looked at each other. Then down at the ground. You could almost hear their thoughts.

Who's going to tell this poor guy that it's too late? That whatever he's going to be, he's already become?

Finally, the princess mustered her courage.

"You're old," she said flatly.

Humbled by a child. Again.

I deserved that one, I guess. To them, I was the size of a giant sequoia and roughly the same age. The idea that I aspired to become something other than what I already was must have seemed odd. I laughed at the exchange but felt a twinge of sadness. *I am old*, I thought. *I'm supposed to have everything figured out by now, but I don't.*

I grew up in the church, and there was a lot of talk about finding God's will for your life. But it was always a young person's sport. In high school, we prayed that God would lead us to the right college or into the right career. As young adults, we prayed for the right spouse, preferably one who was incredibly attractive. There were pitfalls along the way. Finding God's will was a mysterious undertaking—and a delicate one. Don't pray enough and you could miss the boat. Same thing if you sinned too much. And you had to hunt for supernatural clues to find it.

I remember hearing a story (likely apocryphal) about a young man torn over his choice about whom to marry. Should he propose to the lovely Jennifer, or the equally lovely young woman named Joy? Hunting for answers, he flipped open his Bible, right to Isaiah 55:12: "You shall go out with joy."[1] Problem solved.

Such stories struck me as silly. And a lot of what I heard about finding God's will wasn't very helpful. But the focus on calling made sense. At that age, massive, life-altering decisions whip past you like fence posts on the highway. You need guidance. What I didn't realize at the time is that you still need guidance when you're older. The question of what you should do with your life never really goes away. Not completely, anyway. Even after the big puzzle pieces of life fall into place, there are still a lot of blank spots in the picture. The truth is I'm still trying to fill them in.

And I know I'm not alone. I see it in my own family. Grace feels it. After working in the professional world for years, she's now home with the kids. She loves being a mom but admits the change has been disorienting. "My world is very small these days," she says. She longs to use her creative gifts to make an impact on the outside world. As the children grow, she'll have opportunities to do that. But what will it look like? She's not sure.

Or I think of her father, Brian. He's transitioning into retirement. He's been a successful executive in an electronics company for the past thirty-five years. Now he wants to do something completely new. Something that's less about personal success and more about helping others. But he's not quite sure what that will be—and he needs God to guide him.

Even my parents are feeling their way forward. They spent their lives in ministry till my father was forced to retire early because of Parkinson's disease. They still feel called to minister to people, but finding opportunities to do that can be a challenge.

At some point, we all find ourselves uncertain and seeking. The job ends. The kids move out. The relationship shifts. Life changes. And suddenly, you're twenty again, asking, "What now, God?"

BECOME A COMMON CHRISTIAN

In the introduction I recounted how my youthful idealism crashed hard on the rocks of reality. Life was more demanding than I'd anticipated. More exhausting. I also shared how I found the idea of just showing up to be liberating.

What I find freeing about the concept is that it lowers the bar. I can't kill it in every area of life. I can't always be the best. I can't even always be *my* best! But I can be there. I can show up. And, as the saying goes, showing up is 90 percent of success.

But as I sat down to write this book, there was a question nagging me. *Show up for what?* How do we know what God wants us to do in the first place? How do we know what to show up for?

As I reflected on the question, I had a realization. Showing up and finding God's will aren't two separate subjects. In fact, they're closely related.

One thing that simplified the question for me was learning that, as Christians, we all have two callings, not just one.

We have what some have called a *general* or *common* calling. This is what *all* Christians are called to do. When Jesus was asked what the greatest commandment was, He responded by saying, "Love the Lord your God with all your heart and with all your soul and with all your mind" (Matt. 22:37). Then He added this: "This is the first and greatest commandment. And the second is like it: 'Love your neighbor as yourself'" (vv. 38–39). Love God, love others. That's the bottom line. That isn't easy, but we're called to do it. And we don't need signs or a voice from heaven to confirm it. If you're a follower of Jesus, it's part of your common calling.

Every Christian is called to grow in their faith and become more like Jesus. I remember a sermon in which our pastor made a bold declaration: "I know God's will for each person here this morning." That got our attention. Then he quoted 1 Thessalonians 4:3: "It is God's will that you should be sanctified." Holiness, he explained, is not an optional part of the Christian life; it's for everyone. It's part of our common calling.

We also have a *particular* calling. That's the call on your life that applies specifically to you. It involves questions of career. Should you be an electrician or an event planner? A painter or a paralegal? As Westerners, we tend to overemphasize this one, honestly. God cares about your occupation, but I don't think it's His number one concern. And it's not the most important thing about you. The apostle Paul was the greatest missionary of all time. But what was his "job"? He was a tentmaker. That wasn't his primary calling, of course. It just paid the bills.

I'm not saying your career isn't important. It's part of your calling. But so are your relationships. Should you get married?

If so, to whom? Your particular calling also involves *where* you should be. Should you live in Seattle or San Diego? Britain or Bulgaria? The city or the country?

When we talk about God's will, this is the stuff we typically have in mind. These are the questions we lose sleep over and tend to get weird about. We look for signs in the clouds. We examine our dreams. We open our Bible to random pages, hoping for direction.

I recall the story of one woman who was cleaning out her garage when she spotted a spider web in the corner. As she examined the intricate pattern, a thought hit her. God was calling her to design websites (*web*sites, get it?). She had no training as a web designer, but she thought this was a sign. It wasn't. The idea quickly fizzled. It was just a spider web in a garage.

Sometimes we find God's will in strange and dramatic ways. There are plenty of examples of that in Scripture. But I'm convinced that's not how it works for the most part—and that's okay.

Here's the unglamorous truth: Usually, we find God's will as we obey Him. As we act with integrity and faithfulness in our current situation, He lights the path ahead. This is how your *particular* call and *common* call are related. When you focus on fulfilling the common calling, the specific calling of your life has a way of becoming clearer.

Isn't that a relief? You don't have to worry that you're going to miss out on what God wants for you. If you're loving God and loving others, He will guide you. As A. W. Tozer said, the person who is "joyously surrendered to Christ can't make a wrong choice."[2] There's tremendous freedom in that truth.

Even if you're not sure what to do right now, that's okay. You don't need to know what's a hundred miles ahead. God just wants you to take the next step. As pastor Kevin DeYoung advises,

"Don't wait for the liver-shiver. If you are seeking first the kingdom of God and His righteousness, you will be in God's will, so just go out and do something."[3]

TRAINED BY SHEEP

I once got in a weird argument with a friend about Moses. My friend said that the great liberator and lawgiver was inarticulate. I disagreed, insisting the Bible describes him as a man "powerful in speech and action." The problem was this was before the advent of the internet, and I couldn't remember where that appeared in the Bible, so my friend wasn't convinced.

When we finally hunted down the relevant verse, we learned we were both right. Moses is described as being "educated in all the wisdom of the Egyptians . . . powerful in speech and action" (Acts 7:22). Yet when God appears to Moses in Exodus, commanding him to free the Israelites, Moses objects. "I am slow of speech and tongue" (Ex. 4:10).

You can understand our confusion. Moses is described both as slow of speech . . . and powerful in speech. But it's important to note the distance between these descriptions. They capture Moses at different stages of his life. The first is of him as a young man. He's confident, strong, capable of striking down a slave master who was whipping a fellow Israelite. He has a fancy Egyptian education.

The second description comes in a radically different context. It's forty years later, and Moses is an aging shepherd, stuck in the wilderness where he fled after Pharaoh tried to kill him. Now when God shows up and commands Moses to go back to Egypt and liberate the Israelites, Moses is a puddle of fear.

I suppose Moses could have been lying. He clearly doesn't feel up to the job and maybe claiming a lack of rhetorical skill is a ruse to get out of it. But I don't think so. I'm guessing spending forty years tending sheep doesn't do much for your communication abilities. I guess you can talk to sheep, but they're not going to talk back (if they do, you have real problems).

Furthermore, tending sheep isn't exactly glamorous. Sheep are stubborn. Sheep are smelly. And they're not particularly bright. Recently, I saw a viral video clip that hilariously illustrated this fact. In the clip, a sheep is wedged head-down in a crevasse. A young man emerges and patiently, limb by limb, pulls the sheep free. But as soon as the sheep tastes freedom, the animal bounds away—and dives headfirst back into the same crevasse.

Being a shepherd in the ancient world was hard—and boring. It required leading, feeding, watering, and protecting sheep. These activities were punctuated by long periods of inactivity when you just sat, watching over the flock. That's what Moses had been doing for forty years when God shows up. No wonder his verbal skills are a little rusty.

But I believe that the timing of Moses' calling was no accident. God used those years of obscurity to prepare him to lead. Every belligerent sheep he corralled was preparing him to deal with grumbling people. Every predator he fended off was steeling him for the challenge of facing Pharaoh. Each eventless day was building his resolve for a long sojourn in the wilderness. The menial work tamed his pride. The solitude trained him to commune with his Creator. God was forging his character, molding him into the kind of leader he needed to be.

God could have commanded Moses to lead the Israelites to freedom forty years earlier. That's when Moses was at the top of his game. Strong, confident, eloquent. But God's not impressed by such attributes. He didn't need a great orator. He didn't want a talker. He wanted a walker, someone who could lead His people on the long and arduous journey to the promised land. And tending sheep was the perfect training.

I'm sure there were many times when Moses despaired. I'll bet he wondered what was going on with his life. He'd gone from being a prince in Pharaoh's palace to spending decades surrounded by dirty sheep. Maybe he thought God had forgotten about him.

Have you ever wondered that too? Do you ever look at what you're doing right now and ask, *What is God thinking?* Maybe your daily work seems mundane and unimportant. No one appreciates your contributions and you're tired of toiling in obscurity.

If so, I can't tell you exactly what God is up to. But I can tell you this: if you're seeking to honor Him, that work matters. God sees it, even when no one else does. And He's using it in ways you probably don't fully understand right now.

One of those ways is to prepare you for what's next. It may not make sense at the moment, but it will someday. When I look back on my life, I marvel at the odd assortment of jobs I've had. I've sold ice cream and done demolition. I've swept floors and stocked shelves. I've worked in a retirement home and been a caregiver for people with disabilities. I've been a youth pastor and a freelance writer. All these roles helped shape me into the person writing these words right now. It felt a little haphazard

God hasn't forgotten you. Stay faithful. You're not on the shelf. You're in training.

at the time, but I believe God used those experiences to prepare me for the work I'm doing today.

I'm learning that with God, nothing is wasted. Even the failures and setbacks. God uses it all. Those years in the wilderness were crucial to Moses' calling. Just like what you're doing right now is crucial to yours. And in case you're wondering, God hasn't forgotten you. Stay faithful. You're not on the shelf. You're in training.

WALKING IS THE WAY

My friend Dominic Done pointed out something I hadn't noticed about the Bible: it has the word "suddenly" in it a lot. "God is a God of 'suddenly.' It's found 87 [times] in the Bible. They wept, suddenly an angel appeared at the tomb. They walked, suddenly he appeared on the Emmaus road. They prayed, suddenly the Spirit came down."[4]

It's inspiring to think of God suddenly rescuing people or revealing Himself. But I'm struck by what preceded these moments of "sudden" divine intervention: long stretches of quiet faithfulness. The people in these stories were often in the middle of hard or hopeless circumstances. Some were plagued by doubt and despair. But they hadn't given up. They kept going. Praying, weeping, walking. And then, suddenly, God showed up.

That's what happened with Moses. God *suddenly* appears to him, as he's leading sheep.

> Now Moses was tending the flock of Jethro his father-in-law, the priest of Midian, and he led the flock to the far side of the wilderness and came to Horeb, the mountain of God. There the angel of the LORD appeared to him in flames of

> fire from within a bush. . . . God called to him from within the bush, "Moses! Moses!" (Ex. 3:1–4)

Moses had been tending sheep for forty years when this encounter takes place. Forty years of hard, boring work carried out in obscurity. It's only then that God suddenly reveals Moses' unique calling.

That might seem a tad depressing; it is a long time to wait. But ultimately, I think it's encouraging. Moses didn't have to solve a riddle to find God's will for his life. He just had to tend sheep. And in the midst of doing that, God directed him.

It's a good reminder for all of us, especially when we're in a hard or confusing season of life. We can be like Moses, faithfully doing the work God has placed in front of us.

The truth is we don't usually find God's will with our head, or even our hands. We find it with our feet. We keep walking, and as we do, He shows us the path. So, we keep going because we know that God will guide us. We know that plodding leads to prevailing. That steady comes before suddenly. And that when we keep showing up, God does too.

REFLECT

Have you found your "particular" calling? If so, was it a one-time thing or a gradual unfolding? Are you still figuring it out?

Can you look back and see how your past experiences prepared you for what you're doing today? How could that impact the way you encounter future difficulties?

What does it mean to find God's will with your feet? What steps can you take right now to discover where God might be leading you next?

Chapter Four

Be a "Long-Haul Hero"

Invest in Fewer People for Deeper Impact

Eight years ago, I received the worst news of my life. It was sent through Facebook, a surreal way to receive a tragic message.

"Did you hear about Colin?" a friend wrote.

I hadn't. Colin was a close childhood friend. We met in Sunday school as young kids and were inseparable through high school. We both loved sports. I convinced him to leave his first love, hockey, to play basketball. "You're going to be really tall," I told him.

I was right. "Axe," as we all called him (a spin on his last name "Axelsen"), ended up being 6'7". We played on the same team in high school and, later, against each other in college. Ultimately his accomplishments on the hardwood eclipsed mine. I would often remind Axe that he owed me big time for getting him into basketball. "No way," he'd say. "If I would have stuck with hockey, I'd be playing in the NHL right now!"

We stayed in close contact, even after I left Canada for the US. He became a teacher and basketball coach. He and his wife, Leanne, visited Grace and me in just about every place we moved—Pasadena, Orlando, and Chicago. When we started having kids, we shared pictures and stories and even used them to keep our basketball rivalry alive.

"Whose kids do you think will be better ball players?" he asked me.

"Oh, mine for sure," I responded. "They're growing up in the US and will face way better competition."

He wasn't having it.

"Are you kidding me? I'm a coach. Mine will be better for sure!"

As we entered our thirties, we joked around about getting older, about getting fat, about losing hair. We were planning to see each other soon. I told him that after all the trips they'd made to see us, it was our turn to travel north.

Then I got that message. When I responded that I hadn't heard anything, a second message came back.

"Colin and his daughter were killed in a car accident."

I looked at the words on my phone in disbelief. Can't be true. My mind raced. It was too awful to accept. But there was no way our mutual friend would lie about something like this. I was angry that I couldn't argue with what I saw on my phone, that I couldn't find a way to make the short, blunt message staring up at me from my phone untrue. Colin's daughter was a baby, not even a year old. After having two boys, he and Leanne were elated to welcome a little girl. Now she was gone. He was gone, leaving Leanne to raise their two young boys alone.

I received the news while riding in the back of a stranger's car to a speaking engagement. I didn't say anything about it. I was too numb. I felt that if I opened up to this stranger, I might lose it. So, we rode on. I answered questions robotically as the lights on the freeway blurred through my tears.

A week later I traveled home for the funeral. When I walked into the church, I couldn't believe the size of the crowd. Colin lived in a small town in Central Alberta, but the large sanctuary was packed with more than a thousand people. I couldn't even find a seat and ended up standing in the foyer, watching the service on a screen.

As I stood there, my mind drifted back to the many memories of our friendship. I recalled the time we'd met up in Hawaii in our early twenties. After one frustrating day of trying to surf, we sat on the beach, exhausted. As we looked out over the waves, Axe said, "This trip has been great. But more than any of the fun things we've done, it's been awesome getting to hang out with you again. I love you, man."

I shifted awkwardly in the sand. I wasn't quite as emotionally mature as my buddy. "That's a weird thing to say," I said. He laughed. "I know it is," he responded. "But it's true. I love you, buddy."

That's how Axe was. He loved people—and he let them know it.

INFINITE BROWSING MODE

I flew home in a fog of grief. In the subsequent days, I reflected on my friend's short life with sadness but also gratitude. He'd lived well. Colin was a faithful follower of Jesus. He was a loyal son and sibling, a loving husband and father. And he'd left a powerful legacy in the lives of the young students he taught and coached. At his funeral, I got to witness the fruit of that legacy as students lined up to pay homage to the tremendous impact he'd had on their lives.

I also started to think of my own life. What would happen if I were to die in a tragic accident? I knew my family and friends would miss me. But there would be no wider community affected, no line of teary young people lining up to talk about my impact on them. I was a nomad, moving from city to city in pursuit of further education and new jobs. Grace and I had never stayed long in one place. Just when we started making friends, it was off to the next opportunity.

I remember one conversation I had with Axe about his career. He was coaching junior high girls' basketball, and I wondered if maybe his skills would be better used elsewhere. "I'll bet if you made a move, you could be coaching at the college level in a few years," I told him.

He had no interest. "Maybe," he said. "But I love coaching this team. These girls are awesome."

I was taken aback by his response. He'd been a star college player. Now he was a popular teacher and talented coach. He had all kinds of chances for advancement. But he had little interest in opportunities that led him away from the students and community that he loved.

Axe stayed in one place. Put down roots. Invested in the same people for years. Meanwhile, I had moved through the world like a ghost. I'd prioritized opportunities over community, progress over place. There's nothing wrong with pursuing opportunities.

But as I reflected on the hundreds of lives my friend impacted in his short time on the planet, I started to wonder who had taken the better path.

People like Axe are rare these days. We live in a world that encourages restlessness, not rootedness. Fame, not faithfulness. Author Pete Davis compares the experience of browsing Netflix, unable to commit to watching one show, to the way an increasing number of people approach life. "Infinite Browsing Mode" is what he calls it.[1] "I've come to believe that this is the defining characteristic of my generation: *keeping our options open*," he writes.[2]

But Davis notes a growing dissatisfaction with this kind of existence. "As I have grown older, I have become more and more inspired by the people who have clicked out of Infinite Browsing Mode—the people who've chosen a new room, left the hallway, shut the door behind them, and settled in." Davis calls these people he admires "long-haul heroes." He identifies well-known long-haul heroes like Fred Rogers, for "recording 895 episodes of *Mister Rogers' Neighborhood* because he was dedicated to advancing a more humane model of children's television."[3] He also praises lesser known, but no less important people, like his piano teacher, "Mrs. Gatley, who clocked four decades in the same chair next to the same grand piano in her living room on Oak Street."[4]

Trying to do something big can prevent us from showing up for the people right in front of us. Striving to be famous can prevent us from being faithful.

It's easy to see why there are more infinite browsers than long-haul heroes. From the time we're young, we're told, in a million ways, that doing something big will give our lives meaning. It's a message you hear in movies and magazines, at graduation speeches, and even from pulpits. *Go out and do something huge! Change the world!* Even if those words aren't used explicitly, the message is communicated implicitly through inspiring stories of people who overcame all odds to leave their mark on history.

There's nothing wrong with such stories, but I find I'm less inspired by them now. Maybe it's because I'm getting older and worry that my time to make a dramatic impact is running out. Or perhaps it's because I'm starting to realize that they can have a counterproductive effect. Trying to do something big can prevent us from showing up for the people right in front of us. Striving to be famous can prevent us from being faithful. We may influence the wider world. Yet ultimately our greatest contributions will likely be to the lives of the people around us, to our family, friends, and community. The best way to show up for them is by becoming a long-haul hero.

QUIET INFLUENCE

A passage of Scripture that has always struck me as a little strange and, honestly, a tad depressing, is found in 1 Thessalonians 4:11. After commending the Thessalonians for how well they love each other, Paul gives some practical advice: "Make it your ambition to lead a quiet life: You should mind your own business and work with your hands, just as we told you."

The word "ambition" appears only a few places in most translations of the Bible. It's usually in the context of warning against "selfish ambition." Here it's used to urge us to do something that is decidedly unambitious: live a quiet life.

This is jarring to modern readers. In a world obsessed with attention and accolades, it seems downright bizarre to aim for a life that is mundane and modest. Paul would have never made it as a self-help guru. Live a quiet life. Mind your own business. Work with your hands. These words might not sound inspiring, but they are heavy with ancient wisdom. A quiet life is honorable—and keeps you out of trouble. And working diligently (even on mundane tasks) is what ultimately bears fruit. They might not make movies about you, but you'll live a life that matters.

When I edited *Leadership Journal*, a magazine for church leaders, I decided it would be interesting to do a feature asking a handful of prominent pastors who had the greatest influence on their life and ministry. I expected them to respond with a who's who of famous preachers and thinkers. Instead, they wrote about little-known, faithful servants who had invested in them early in their careers. Dan Darling recalled the impact of a pastor named Bill Swanger. "He didn't have a platform. . . . He didn't write any books or have a large social media following. Bill was, quite simply, a shepherd."[5] And he shepherded Darling.

> I distinctly remember a time when I faced some hard decisions that I didn't want to make. I complained about having to deal with them. Bill gently said, "Dan, this is part of your calling. This is what we do. You have to dig in and do it." He was right. We don't pastor for the perks or the position or the popularity. We pastor because God has called us to this and because we love people.[6]

The roundup contained many other similar stories. Usually the person they cited sought them out when they were young and built into their lives in a meaningful way. These mentors were wise and patient. They stuck by them through difficult seasons, counseled them, loved them. I didn't recognize one of their names.

If you do end up having a broader impact, it will likely come from investing in the lives of a small number of people.

Opting for quiet influence can feel like settling. For people raised on a steady drumbeat of self-help aphorisms and get-famous stories, it can even seem like a sort of death.

Maybe you fear that investing in a small number of people means kissing any chance at broader influence goodbye. But that isn't the case. The truth is, if you do end up having a broader impact, it will likely come from investing in the lives of a small number of people. When you look at virtually any movement or ideology, from the arts to abolition, the ideas that broke out and affected the masses were incubated in small groups of passionate people. They often emerged in the context of white-hot community, and then branched off to change the world. As Margaret Mead famously said, "Never doubt that a small group of thoughtful, committed citizens can change the world; indeed, it's the only thing that ever has."[7]

Think of the early church. It started as a tiny, marginalized Jewish offshoot consisting mostly of illiterate slaves. But they gained a reputation for their unusual love and compassion. The pagan emperor Julian railed against "these impious Galileans [Christians] who not only feed their own poor, but ours also, welcoming them into their *agape*."[8] Julian's fears were well-founded. Within three hundred years of the church's founding, the majority of the Roman Empire would be Christian.

Of course, for the ultimate example of the power of a narrow focus, we must go back even earlier. Nothing demonstrates this better than the life and ministry of Jesus. Yes, He spoke to the crowds, but He spent most of His time with just twelve friends. When I visited Israel and toured the sites described in the New Testament, I was struck by how tiny the scope was geographically. Our guide cited a statistic that blew me away: nearly all of Jesus' ministry took place within a physical space of about ten square miles.

SCALING BACK

I have too many people in my life. I'm betting you do too. If you add up the connections from childhood, high school, college, sports teams, past hobbies, past jobs, past churches, places you used to live, I'm guessing it adds up to hundreds, if not *thousands* of people. A handful of those connections are still strong. Maybe you check in occasionally by grabbing coffee or giving them a call. Other relationships you've let wither, perhaps with some feelings of regret. Those relationships are not completely dead, but not fully alive, either. They're zombie friendships, staggering to life occasionally via social media notices of life updates, like graduations, marriages, job changes, and cancer diagnoses. The sad thing is that you were once close to many of these people. And you feel a pang of guilt when you think of how long it's been since you've spoken to them.

We have far more friends than our ancestors did. We move more and travel more, picking up friends from all over the country and even different parts of the world. And thanks to the advent of social media, we're now digitally connected to people we've never even met in real life.

If it all feels like too much, it's probably because it is. In the 1990s, the British anthropologist Robin Dunbar proposed that we're only truly capable of having about 150 friends. Dunbar, who studied nonhuman primates, extrapolated his findings for humans and came up with his now-famous number. He also noted that historically a lot of social groups, from medieval villages to residential campsites, tend to have around 150 people. Some anthropologists have objected to Dunbar's number. But whatever the ideal number of friends, it likely doesn't come close to the thousands of connections our hyper-mobile, hyper-connected lives have bestowed on us.

Our bloated networks also strain our empathy. Recently Grace and I talked about how we felt overwhelmed by all the pain we encounter online. She'd read a Facebook post about how one person (a friend of a friend) had lost a child. I'd seen a post from a colleague I'd worked with fourteen years ago who had been diagnosed with a serious illness. Another friend, that I barely knew in high school, announced that her marriage had ended. That was just a sampling of the stories we'd seen; there were dozens of others.

We realized that before social media we likely would have never heard about one of these awful developments. And it was taking a toll on our mental health. We felt bad for feeling bad. After all, the burden of knowing about these losses was nothing compared to what each of these people was going through. But we wondered if we were really meant to be exposed to a constant barrage of bad news and tragedy. Sure, we could pray and offer condolences, but usually we were too far from the situation to do anything else. It was all too much, especially when added to the steady stream of catastrophe, tragedy, and outrage we get from the news. As pastor Glenn Packiam put it, "When our awareness outpaces our agency, we are left with anxiety."[9]

Rather than amplifying our empathy, constant exposure to tragedy can numb you. Furthermore, it's easy to fool yourself into thinking you helped because you liked a post or left a broken heart emoji. And it can make you less likely to help those in your immediate vicinity. C. S. Lewis warned about this dynamic.

> I think each village was meant to feel pity for its own sick and poor whom it can help and I doubt if it is the duty of any private person to fix his mind on ills which he cannot help. This may even become an escape from the works of charity we really can do to those we know. God may call any one of us to respond to some far away problem or support those who have been so called. But we are finite, and he will not call us everywhere or to support every worthy cause. And real needs are not far from us.[10]

Lewis wrote those words in the middle of the twentieth century. Just imagine what he'd say if he could see our world today. Now, 24-hour cable news and social media drive us to invest our attention in the lives of strangers while ignoring the needs in our own backyard.

We have limited time and attention and energy. And the people God has placed in front of us deserve the lion's share of it.

I'm learning that it's okay to fight this tendency and narrow your scope of concern. That it isn't callous. It's acknowledging reality. As Lewis said, we are finite, and God doesn't expect us to respond to every problem. We have limited time and attention and energy. And the people God has placed in front of us deserve the lion's share of it.

WHAT MATTERS IN THE END?

When I was in my twenties, I worked at an assisted living facility. Most of the residents were in their eighties and nineties and had serious physical limitations. I was the activity director (actually, I was the *assistant* to the activity director). But I was responsible for setting up events to keep the seniors engaged.

One day, I had a brilliant idea. They were shut up in this rather depressing place and many had no idea what was going on in the outside world. So, I decided I would read the newspaper headlines to them and open a discussion on current events.

It didn't work.

I'd gather them in a circle, open the day's newspaper, and read a headline.

"Violence Breaks Out in the Middle East!"

Silence. I'd try again.

"Oh, this is interesting. They landed a rover on Mars!"

More silence.

When I asked what they thought about the day's news, they were less than enthusiastic. They'd wave the headlines away and say things like, "Who cares?!" "It doesn't matter!" or "You're too loud!" (Call me sensitive but I couldn't help but take that last one personally.)

They didn't give a rip about the news.

I decided to scrap it and started a different activity I called "True Stories." It was simple. I just opened the floor and invited them to share stories about their lives.

And boy, did they have them! One man recounted having lunch with Eleanor Roosevelt. He sat to the right of the First Lady but was confused that she wouldn't respond to his questions. Only later did he learn that she was deaf in her right ear and likely hadn't heard him. Another resident chuckled recalling her brother's drinking problem. He would go to the saloon in town; afterward, he'd climb into his horse-drawn carriage and pass out, but the horses would bring him home, unconscious but safe, every night. One man recalled how he had to start working at eleven years old when his older brothers left to fight in the war. "World War II?" I asked him. "No, that was the first one," he said.

During our last "True Stories" session, a wizened farmer reminisced about the first date with his wife. They were both sixteen. He smiled as he described her waiting outside her house in a flower dress, and bobby pins in her hair. He picked her up to go dancing. "I've been picking her up ever since," he said and started to cry. She'd been taken into the hospital earlier in the week after suffering a massive stroke, from which she later died.

There was a lot of crying and laughing in that room—often at the same time. I just listened, honored to hear their stories.

What's my point? Simply this: think about what will matter in the end.

Those seniors helped me do that. My friend Colin did too.

Right now, you might be bent on changing the world or becoming a big deal. But I can promise that when you come to the end of your life, that's not what you'll care about. You won't be worried about how successful you were or how much money you made. You certainly won't care about the news. The macro stories won't matter much. The micro ones will. You'll remember who you invested in and who invested in you. You'll be thinking about how well you loved the people God placed in your life. You'll be glad you showed up.

REFLECT

Do you know any "long-haul heroes"? What enabled them to invest deeply in people?

What does it mean to "lead a quiet life"? How might that enable you to better pursue your calling and bless others?

Have you felt overwhelmed by the sheer amount of information and tragedy you're exposed to online? How can you protect your time and compassion reserves so you're able to be present to the people around you?

Chapter Five

Play the Role

Because People Need You To

We named our son Athanasius. As you might guess, we didn't pick that one out of a baby name book. He was named after the fourth-century church father Athanasius of Alexandria.

It's a big name—and not an easy one to pronounce. You should hear the many commendable yet ill-fated attempts people make at saying it. "He goes by 'Athan,'" I tell strangers, hoping to spare them the ordeal of stumbling through the pronunciation. "Oh, like the city in Greece," they proclaim. *Not really*, I think. But at that point, I don't want to cause any more confusion. I'm the one who gave my kid a weird name, after all.

I encountered the original Athanasius in seminary. I remember reading about how, at a young age, he argued persuasively for the divinity of Jesus at the Council of Nicaea. Athanasius articulated what came to be embraced as the church's official position on Christ's identity, and he spent the rest of his life defending it, often in the teeth of violent opposition.

I was captivated by his unswerving passion for truth. His contemporaries dubbed him *Athanasius, Contra Mundum*, Latin for "Athanasius against the world." He refused to compromise his beliefs, even when it meant clashing with Roman emperors. By the end of his life, he'd been exiled five times.

I came home from my church history class one day and told Grace, "If we ever have a son, I want to name him after this guy." Somehow, she agreed. When our son was born, Athanasius it was.

It's too early to know if my son will become a great defender of the faith, but in at least one way he already matches his namesake perfectly. He's stubborn! Sometimes it's good, like the time he called out an older boy for saying something racist. Other times it's not so good—and he gets exiled to his bedroom.

A few years ago, I overheard him in a heated argument with his sister.

"You listen to ME!" he shouted at her. "I was named after a very important Christian!"

That's when I decided to intervene.

"Hey, bud, are you sure you want to play that card? On your sister . . . Mary?"

Even he had to laugh.

ROLE CALL

My son's name seems to fit. My prayer is that, like the original Athanasius, he'll learn to use his iron will for the right things. I hope he will grow into his name.

We grow into a lot of things in life. Sometimes it's a name. Drew means "strong and manly," so yeah, my parents nailed it. Other times we grow into a role we're given. Like names, they're often given to us before we fully understand them. Son. Daughter. Brother. Sister. Friend. Student. We enter each of these with little knowledge of what they mean or require. But that's what living is for. Eventually, we learn how to play these roles. And they, in turn, shape us. They give our lives substance. They become the forms into which we are poured.

Speaking of roles in a positive way sounds strange, especially to those of us raised in the highly individualistic culture of the West. We grew up on stories about throwing off socially assigned roles and asserting our autonomy. We were taught to follow our hearts, be rebels, and resist conformity. As a result, playing a role can feel boring, even dishonest. But I'm convinced we need to get more comfortable with the idea.

In the last chapter, we learned about being a "long-haul hero," someone who resists the temptation to keep their options endlessly open and commits to a particular path. When you do that, something wonderful and scary happens. God leads you into new roles. People start to trust you, lean on you, look to you for leadership. That's the wonderful part. The scary part? People start to trust you, lean on you, look to you for leadership. Sometimes we're reluctant to take these roles on. Maybe we see them as too restrictive. Roles demand another level of commitment. They come with new responsibilities. That can be difficult to accept, especially for people conditioned by individualism.

Another reason roles freak us out? We feel inadequate, unprepared. Remember our discussion of Moses? God used his experience as a shepherd to prepare him to lead Israel. Yet when God calls Moses to his new role, he shrinks back, convinced he's the wrong person for the job.

We do that too. God opens an opportunity to don a new role,

but we resist. We claim we're the wrong person or say it's too hard. It's a shame, because it's often through these roles that we fulfill God's call on our lives.

Roles are good. They are frameworks for influence. They enable us to lead, encourage, equip, instruct, and inspire people. They help us leverage the gifts God's given us to bless the world. Showing up for others usually means owning a role. Even if it feels a little weird at first.

AUTHENTICITY ISN'T EVERYTHING

As I mentioned in the last chapter, I used to work as an editor on a magazine for church leaders. I was in my early thirties at the time, and my boss, Marshall Shelley, was from a different generation. He had led the magazine for nearly as long as I'd been alive.

I remember sitting in a planning meeting where we discussed doing a whole issue of the magazine on the theme of authenticity. It had become a buzzword in ministry circles. There was no denying that people seemed to connect with pastors who opened up with congregants, sharing their personal struggles and shortcomings.

I was excited about the idea, as was another thirtysomething colleague. But Marshall shrugged. He saw the need for authenticity in leadership but felt it should be balanced by a sense of duty. "Sometimes pastors need to ignore their feelings," he said. "They need to set aside whatever might be going on in their personal lives and just perform the role people need from them."

The statement sounded like heresy to me. I chalked it up to the old-school thinking of a man nearly my father's age. Surely ignoring your feelings was unhealthy. Plus, wasn't it dishonest to get up in front of people and perform a role when your heart wasn't really in it?

Soon after that meeting, however, I had an experience that made me admit he had a point. Grace was in the hospital recovering from a surgery. She was fine but we were a little shaken by the ordeal. We needed someone to come alongside us in that moment. We were grateful when one of the pastors from our church dropped by. But the visit was different than I'd anticipated.

Sometimes it's good to play a role, even when your heart isn't in it.

After a perfunctory greeting, he plunked himself down in the chair next to Grace's bed and stared at the floor. "Guys, things aren't going so well," he confessed. "Sometimes I don't even know why I'm in ministry." He proceeded to tell us about various problems the church was facing and aired doubts over his ability to handle them. He was very authentic and transparent (probably too transparent), but it wasn't what we needed in that moment. We needed someone to come into that room and pray for us, reassure us. We needed a pastor.

I learned a valuable lesson that day. Sometimes it's good to play a role, even when your heart isn't in it. That's not only true of pastors. We all have certain roles in life. And sometimes effectively performing those roles demands setting our feelings aside. That doesn't mean we're duplicitous. We don't want to ignore or stifle our feelings. But, at times, we're required to act in spite of them. That may not be pleasant but it's important. Why? Because people are counting on us.

ROLE PLAYING

Most roles feel a little weird at first. Like a new pair of shoes, they take a while to break in. When Grace and I first got married, it was wonderful but strange. We were young and joked on more than one occasion about how it felt like we were "playing house." We'd laugh a little when we referred to each other as husband or wife. I'd walk through the door and dramatically announce, "Honey, I'm home!" even though I was only returning from a two-hour college class, not a full day of work like a *real* husband. It was the same when we had kids. I remember nervously strapping my son into his car seat for the first time. I didn't feel like a dad. I felt like I was stealing a baby from the hospital!

Yet today, these roles feel natural. In fact, it would feel weird *not* being a husband or father. They've become part of my identity. It's taken practice, sacrifice, and (honestly) a lot of messing up before I learned to fill these roles well. But if I would have waited until I was fully prepared to be a husband or father, it never would have happened.

It's like that with a lot of roles. Initially, they feel foreign, scary. And that can keep you from stepping into them. Have you felt this? Maybe there is a role you've been eyeing but something seems to be holding you back. Perhaps you're convinced you're not old enough or smart enough or spiritual enough to pursue it. Or maybe you're already in a role but find yourself haunted by what they call "imposter syndrome," that nagging fear that you're not good enough and it's just a matter of time before everyone finds out.

If so, I have great news. You're probably not good enough—but that's okay. I'm not saying that qualifications and preparation aren't important. But we never feel fully equipped and prepared.

So, you can't let feelings of inadequacy stop you. At some point you have to step forward and play the role, knowing you're going to stumble your way through.

The even better news is that Scripture is jammed with people just like us. The Bible tells story after story of people taking on roles despite overwhelming feelings of inadequacy. Yet God called them to their roles (downright badgered them in some cases) knowing that the grace and power the roles required would be provided along the way.

Let's talk about Moses again. We looked at how God appears to him in the burning bush and commands him to lead the Israelites out of Egypt. Moses doesn't doubt God; the encounter was undeniable. But he doubts himself. "Pardon your servant, Lord. I have never been eloquent, neither in the past nor since you have spoken to your servant. I am slow of speech and tongue" (Ex. 4:10).

The bizarre thing about Moses' response is that it comes *after* God gives him two miraculous signs to confirm his calling. On God's orders, Moses has just thrown his staff on the ground and watched it transform into a snake. He's seen his hand struck with leprosy—then instantly restored to health. Given the dramatic display of power that precedes it, Moses' refusal to step into his role is almost comedic in its absurdity. Does he really think that the God of the universe, who has just demonstrated His complete power over nature, somehow accidentally picked the wrong guy to fulfill His mission?

I find it interesting how God responds to Moses' refusal to lead. He doesn't give him a pep talk. He doesn't remind Moses of his first-rate Egyptian education or praise his rhetorical abilities. Instead, He reminds Moses of who came up with the idea of speech in the first place. "Who gave human beings their mouths?"

God responds. "Who makes them deaf or mute? Who gives them sight or makes them blind? Is it not I, the LORD? Now go; I will help you speak and will teach you what to say" (Ex. 4:11–12).

I love that. It means when God calls you to do something, His abilities matter more than yours. The One who sends is more important than the one who goes. It's not really about you.

Isn't that freeing? It makes it much easier to step forward in faith, knowing that God's ability to use you doesn't rest on your fragile shoulders.

FUTURE YOU

Here's another encouraging truth. God sees the future. Which means He doesn't see you only as you are right now. He also sees what you will one day become.

Consider the story of Gideon in the book of Judges. Gideon is called into a new role at a time when the Israelites are in a crisis. They've abandoned the worship of God and they are being terrorized by their enemies, the Midianites. They live in constant fear, hiding out in caves. That's when an angel of the Lord appears. He tells Gideon, "The LORD is with you, valiant warrior" and commands him to "save Israel from the hand of Midian" (Judg. 6:12, 14 NASB).

Gideon is baffled. The grand greeting and bold mission both seem absurd. "How can I save Israel?" he asks. "My clan is the weakest in Manasseh, and I am the least in my family" (Judg. 6:15).

In other words, he tells the angel he's in no position to lead. Valiant warrior? He's the youngest member of the weakest family in one tribe of a conquered people. God has the wrong guy. Like Moses, Gideon requires a series of miraculous signs to confirm the calling. But he finally obeys and leads the Israelites to one of the most improbable victories in the whole Bible, defeating the entire Midianite army with only three hundred men.

Turns out Gideon was a valiant warrior after all. He couldn't see it at first. But God did.

We tend to bestow titles on people only after they've earned them. You're not the boss till you get the promotion. You don't get to be the "champ" until you've beaten the best. But God seems to delight in reversing the order, and "calls into being things that were not" (Rom. 4:17). He looks at shepherds and calls them leaders. He points at wimps and calls them warriors.

Or at a waffling coward and calls him a rock. That's what happened when Jesus renamed His disciple Simon "Peter," which means "the rock." That must have made the other disciples laugh. Peter was bombastic and indecisive. He could be swinging a sword at a soldier one moment, then backing down to a servant girl the next. He boasted that he would die alongside Jesus—then chickened out and fled when the moment arrived. Peter was anything but rocklike. But Jesus looked beyond his foibles and saw the person he would one day become. It took years, but Peter eventually lived up to that name. He faithfully led the first church in Rome and was eventually martyred for his faith. He became the rock that Jesus knew he would be.

He doesn't usually deliver the message through a burning bush or angelic messenger, but He still speaks. And often He does so by revealing the needs around you.

I hope that's encouraging to you. It should be. It means that God looks at you, with all your insecurities and weaknesses, with all your past mistakes and current flaws—and still calls you to step into roles to serve Him and bless others.

He doesn't usually deliver the message through a burning bush or angelic messenger, but He still speaks. And often He does so by revealing the needs around you.

I like what author Heather Thompson says about the topic. In her book *I'll See You Tomorrow*, Thompson recounts her hellish first year in college. Her friends turned on her and she ended up calling her mom in the middle of the night, crying, "Please, come get me."[1] The experience was so awful that she ended up quitting the track team and dropping out of college.

Today, Thompson is a professor who has a heart for hurting students. "When a college freshman cries in my office, I don't roll my eyes," she writes. "I know what those tears feel like."[2] She sees a direct line between her painful experience in college and the work she does now. And she has some great advice for the rest of us. "If you want to know where God may be calling you, look back. What gaps did you fall in? How can you fill them so someone else doesn't?"[3]

Noticing needs can help you find your role—and help you to perform it. Grace shared a tip with me that she's found helpful. "Whenever I'm feeling nervous about performing a certain role, I just ask, 'What do people need from me in this situation?' That takes the focus off me and lets their needs direct my actions."

That's good advice. Thinking about your own qualifications and performance is paralyzing. Better to spin the spotlight around, off yourself and onto others. Then you can see clearly how to help.

Grace is a wise woman, which she proved yet again recently when I came to her with something I was worried about. Our son had been spending a lot of time with a group of boys in the neighborhood. I was happy that he'd found some buddies, but I was concerned they could be a bad influence on him. A few of the kids came from homes where the parents seemed to let them do just about anything. One of the boys had a father who was in jail. I felt bad for these kids, and a little sheepish for even voicing my concerns to Grace. But I was worried for our son. "Maybe we should tell him that we don't want him hanging out with them so much," I suggested.

Grace shared my concern but saw a different solution. "Maybe we're thinking about this the wrong way," she told me. "What if instead of viewing those boys as a threat to our son, you saw them as an opportunity? What if they were placed in our neighborhood so you could be a sort of father figure to them and help fill in what's missing in their lives?"

Ouch. I knew she was right. Fear had distorted my thinking, preventing me from seeing a great opportunity to help kids who desperately needed it. It took Grace nudging me past fear to see the situation through the eyes of faith.

I'm glad that Grace did that for me. Now let me do the same for you.

Has God brought a need to your attention? Have you felt a faint tug toward a new role? And even though you may have held back because of fear, you knew deep down that God was calling you to it?

If so, don't hang back. Step into it. Be that person. Play the role. Be the mentor. The teacher. The coach. The leader. The encourager. The friend. You may feel unequal to the task. But don't look at your résumé. Look to God. He's calling you, valiant warrior. With Him, you can do anything.

REFLECT

How do you view roles? Do you see them as confining, or liberating? Have you ever taken a role that felt scary at first but ended up being a great fit?

Can you identify with how reluctant Bible characters like Gideon and Moses felt about filling the roles God called them to? What do their stories teach us about how we should respond when God directs us to a new role?

Professor Heather Thompson recommends looking back to see what gaps you fell into and then asking, "How can you fill them so someone else doesn't?" How can your past struggles shape the roles you take to help others?

Chapter Six

Just Crack Open Your Bible

Even When You Don't Feel Like It

I used to memorize as many as twenty Bible verses a day. I memorized the book of James, then Romans. Next, I tackled Acts. I didn't manage to conquer all twenty-eight chapters of Luke's history of the early church, but I did commit large swaths of it to memory.

Before you get too impressed, I should let you in on a secret. I did all of this at a time in my life when I had no job, no bills, and virtually no responsibilities.

I was twelve years old.

I was part of my church's Bible Quizzing program. We'd memorize large portions of Scripture, then travel to "quiz meets" to compete against other adolescents on how much we could recall. These events had the feel of a sports tournament. We'd sit in a line before a judge who would call out a Bible passage. "James 2:13!" The first quizzer to stand would get to recite the verse. Or the judge would start reading a verse and the first one off their chair would get a chance to complete it. If we recited the passage "word perfect," we were awarded one point. The first quizzer to get four points won the match.

I wish I could say I was motivated to memorize the Bible out of a deep desire to know God. The truth was less admirable. I wanted to win trophies and impress girls. I didn't have a full appreciation for what I was learning. My knack for memorizing galloped past my ability to understand. I remember at one quiz meet tripping over the word "propitiation" as I quoted Romans 3:25. I knew the word but had no idea what it meant.

Yet even so, to this day, I'm grateful for the experience. It was a gift to internalize so much of God's Word at a young age, even though it would take years to truly grasp the meaning of what I'd learned.

STARTING SMALL

My relationship to Scripture is a lot different now. Back then I paid little attention to the content of what I was reading. Now I try to dwell on Scripture, reading it slowly, letting it read me. But my ability to memorize is a joke. At twelve, my brain was a sponge, effortlessly soaking up thousands of words. Now I rarely try to memorize the Bible. When I do, it is painstaking. The words stay on the page. It's like my brain is folding its arms and shaking its head. "Sorry . . . we have too many words in here already."

But the biggest difference? I have way less time to read my Bible. My days start with kids running into my room and jumping on my bed (I don't remember the last time I slept long enough to hear my alarm go off). Then I reach for my phone and see my inbox brimming with new emails, each one a request that will demand my time and attention.

The day passes in a blur of tasks and meetings. Then the evening is spent with family. By the time Grace and I go through the grueling nighttime routine I described in the introduction, I'm spent. I usually have a couple of hours free before going to bed, but can I confess something super unspiritual? Watching Netflix is more entertaining than reading Leviticus. Scrolling on my phone is much easier than spending time in prayer. If I haven't carved out time to spend with God earlier in the day, it won't happen then.

Recently I was scrolling on my phone when I probably should have been reading my Bible. I came across an internet meme that had two pictures. In the first frame was a picture of a dog with the caption: "This dog has been trained to find people who haven't been reading their Bibles." In the second frame, the dog's nose takes up the entire picture, sniffing you out. Busted.

I laughed—and kept scrolling.

For a long time, I felt bad about my anemic engagement with Scripture. I'd look over at my big, black Bible on my dresser gathering dust and cringe. It was a sore spot in my mind, a source of guilt and regret. It was little comfort to consider that I'm not alone. Though Americans have a ton of Bibles (three Bibles per home on average), we by and large don't read them. Of the people who do report reading their Bible, the majority (58 percent) only do so four times a year or less.[1]

Those statistics include a lot of people who don't even identify as believers. I've dedicated my life to following Jesus. I believe the Bible is the Word of God! How could I fail to even read it?

The solution for me wasn't cranking my motivation up to new heights. Strangely, the breakthrough came when I lowered the bar.

We often think we must dedicate large portions of time to read the Bible or somehow it doesn't count. Ditto for other spiritual practices. We assume we need to pray for an hour a day. Or fast for weeks. Or go on a silent retreat. Or master an exotic spiritual discipline with a Latin name.

These are all great ideas, but I've discovered something liberating. Just as we saw with finding our calling, when it comes to communing with God, it's okay to start small. An all-or-nothing approach blinds us to the fact that there are tremendous benefits to even talking to God for a few minutes or reading a verse or two of Scripture. The secret is to be consistent. Over time you build habits that strengthen your spiritual muscles and deepen your relationship with God.

PRAYER AND PUSH-UPS

One common reaction when you fail to spend time with God? You just give up. Throw in the towel. Call it quits. Feeling guilty gets old. Conceding defeat is no fun, but it beats living in that no-man's-land between faithfulness and failure. You start to wonder if it's all that important anyway. *Is it really necessary to read from a big ancient book every day? Does God care whether I talk to Him regularly? Isn't that just legalism?*

It can be. If you feel like God's going to zap you for missing your daily devotions, you've probably got some legalism issues (and maybe a touch of OCD). Neglecting spiritual disciplines doesn't hurt God. It hurts you. You sever yourself from the nourishment your soul needs. And like any nourishment, spiritual or physical, consistency is key.

I remember my pastor explaining this concept with an analogy. He asked us to imagine being a person who eats junk food all the time and never exercises (some of us didn't have to imagine very hard). Then the day before going to the doctor for a checkup, you eat a salad and go for a run. "How much difference would that make in your checkup?" he asked. Not much. One day of healthy eating and exercise isn't going to offset years of sitting on the couch eating Doritos. But if you'd been living a healthy lifestyle for the past six months, then it starts to make an impact. Do it for a year, and you'll see major changes. Maybe instead of getting a lecture from your doctor during your next appointment, you'll get a pat on the back.

It's the same with spiritual health, he said. Reading your Bible once or twice won't make a huge difference in your life. But the daily practice of spending time with God changes you in the long run. Over time, practices like prayer and Bible reading nourish your soul. They strengthen your connection to God. Eventually, they help forge the kind of faith that can withstand the storms of life.

Pastor Josh Howerton recounted that he and an older man in his life were facing a difficult situation together. Josh, a young pastor, was flustered by the situation but the older man was not shaken. "You have more faith than me," Josh told the man. "No," the man responded. "I have more experience with a faithful God."[2] That kind of faith doesn't come from getting the occasional spiritual high. It comes from years of walking with God.

The practice of walking with God doesn't always feel exhilarating. In fact, it can feel rather mundane. My friend Kyle Rohane had a childhood pastor who continued to mentor him as an adult. He advised Kyle to make his quiet time a priority. "Do it first thing, before your mind gets cluttered. Start with ten minutes a day or even less. How you choose to spend the time is up to you. Find a favorite place. Meet the Lord in the same place every day."

The mentor stressed that consistency was key. "It's like doing push-ups," he told Kyle. "It transforms us. Over the years it shapes us, shapes our lives, shapes our theology and all our relationships."

At first, Kyle balked at the push-up language. "That felt like such a cold, strange description to me. How can you treat time with God as a rote routine (like doing push-ups) while expecting it to be a warm, organic relationship?"

But he came to see the wisdom in his mentor's approach. "It took me a while to understand what he meant, but he was right. Intentional repetition creates the space for that relationship to flourish. It's about familiarity. The repetition keeps the relationship warm. It grows cold when we fall out of the habit."

Tish Harrison Warren makes a similar point in *Liturgy of the Ordinary*. "I often want to skip the boring, daily stuff to get to the thrill of an edgy faith." Yet she found there's no shortcut to spiritual vitality. "The kind of spiritual life and disciplines needed to sustain the Christian life are quiet, repetitive, and ordinary."[3]

It's easy to pray and read your Bible when you're feeling inspired. I'll hear a powerful sermon on Sunday and vow to spend each morning that week with God. But I wake up on Monday morning only to find my inspiration has evaporated. Maybe it's the pile of weekly responsibilities looming or the fact that I'm just not a morning person. But I no longer feel that desire to connect with my Creator. To push through and do so can almost feel wrong. *Should I really pray when my heart isn't in it? Should I try to spend time with God when I'm not feeling inspired?*

It's the very act of showing up and seeking God that often generates feelings that weren't present to begin with.

In a word, yes. Eugene Peterson writes, "Feelings are great liars. If Christians worshiped only when they felt like it, there would be precious little worship."[4] That doesn't mean feelings are unimportant. Or that we're doomed to slog through spiritual practices without inspiration. But it's the very act of showing up and seeking God that often generates feelings that weren't present to begin with.

Again, Peterson is helpful: "We think that if we don't *feel* something there can be no authenticity in *doing* it. But the wisdom of God says something different: that we can *act* ourselves into a new way of feeling much quicker than we can *feel* ourselves into a new way of acting."[5]

We understand this dynamic in every other area of life. If you want to become a star runner, but run only when you feel energetic, it will never happen. If you want to learn chess, but give up the moment you're frustrated or confused, you will never become more than a novice. If you're only romantic with your partner when you're feeling passionate, you will never have a healthy marriage. The spiritual life is no different. Often, we must act in the absence of feelings. And taking action is hard. They are called spiritual *disciplines* for a reason. They take discipline.

But here's the good news. It's worth it. When we regularly commune with God, we grow. To use the biblical language, we discover for ourselves that "[God] rewards those who earnestly seek him" (Heb. 11:6) and that we "reap a harvest" if we do not "weary of doing good" (Gal. 6:9).

SPIRITUAL INCREMENTALISM

Spiritual disciplines should be consistent. That's not controversial. But this next bit of advice might be. *Make them small.* Don't try to do too much. Just open your Bible once a day. Say a quick prayer each morning. Spend five minutes in silence with God.

A couple years ago, my friend Jeremy shared his frustration over not being able to implement a spiritual discipline. "For a long time, I've been trying to spend an hour every day memorizing Scripture," he said. "But I never seem to be able to do it."

I think I laughed out loud. An hour of Bible memorization every day? Talk about starting in the deep end! I knew enough about his life to realize just how unrealistic this goal was. In addition to having three kids and a demanding job, he helps his wife run a growing ballet company. Memorizing the Bible for an hour a day was a pipe dream.

Even moderately ambitious plans have a way of flopping. A lot of people try to read the whole Bible every year. It's a laudable goal! And there are great resources out there to help you do it.[6] But the vast majority fail. And they beat themselves up when they do. They feel like failures, especially when they're still reading January's passages when June rolls around. What should be a source of nourishment and joy becomes a source of quiet shame. Reading the Bible in a year is certainly doable. It takes about fifteen to twenty minutes per day. But even that may be too ambitious at first.

Part of the problem is that when we dive into spiritual disciplines, we fail to account for a simple truth of human psychology.

We're creatures of habit. What is a habit? According to Charles Duhigg, author of *The Power of Habit*, "a habit is a behavior that starts as a choice, and then becomes a nearly unconscious pattern."[7] As you repeat a behavior enough, something changes at the neurological level. The behavior literally wears a rut in your mind. "Neurons that fire together wire together," say brain scientists. The result? Over time, what once took effort and intention becomes almost effortless and automatic. If you develop good habits, they can carry you. You don't have to think too much or try too hard. You just do it.

But here's the catch. Habits have the best chance of sticking when they start *small*. New behaviors are hard and awkward. You haven't worn that rut in your brain yet. It takes lots of willpower and concentration. If you start big, you make it even more difficult and almost impossible to sustain the behavior through the crucial window of habit formation.[8] But starting small gives you the best chance of making the habit stick.

Starting small is counterintuitive. When you're motivated to change your life, you want to make big, sweeping changes. But in a cruel twist of irony, you end up sabotaging your chance at implementing real change because you're almost sure to give up before a habit can take root. That's why starting small is so crucial. James Clear, author of *Atomic Habits*, writes, "People often think it's weird to get hyped about reading one page or meditating for one minute. . . . But the point is not to do one thing. The point is to master the habit of showing up. The truth is, a habit must be established before it can be improved."[9]

If you doubt this is how good habits form, just think about *bad* habits. Say you're addicted to social media. I'm guessing the first time you opened Facebook or Instagram, you didn't spend hours scrolling. You probably created an account, poked around a little, then left. Maybe you wondered what all the fuss was about and doubted whether you'd even be back. But you started checking in occasionally. Then you got used to that small jolt of satisfaction from someone "liking" your post or picture. After a while, you opened the app more regularly. Then one day you wake up to the sad realization that you're frittering away hours a day scrolling. You have a big problem. But it started small.

Fortunately, you can use this same principle to instill good habits. This is why behavioral experts recommend doing bizarrely small tasks, like flossing one tooth each day or just putting on your running shoes.[10] Seems silly, but there's a method to their madness. They know that flossing one tooth or lacing up your sneakers is easy. And if it's easy, you will continue doing it. And if you continue doing it, it will become a habit. Soon you'll be flossing all your teeth and going for that run. BJ Fogg, founder of the Behavior Design Lab at Stanford University, explains it this way: "The *easier* a behavior is to do, the more *likely* the behavior will become a habit."[11]

LITTLE BY LITTLE

I wrote more extensively on habits in my last book, and some readers pushed back. We don't need to understand habits to live the Christian life, they said. I get the objection. After all, Christians got by without it for almost two thousand years. But why not use our knowledge of how God made us? After all, when we talk about things like habits, we're just naming processes God designed.

Starting small is simply about giving yourself the best chance at establishing holy habits in your life. Over time, small practices can lead to big changes. Just imagine if you woke up every morning and felt an inner tug to open God's Word. What if you couldn't go to sleep without spending some time in prayer? What if your day didn't feel right until you'd spent some time in silence with your Creator?

The Desert Fathers were early Christian hermits who fled to the wild in order to live a purer form of faith. They were known for their asceticism. Many fasted for weeks, gave away all their possessions, and prayed for hours every day. But it was Saint Basil, the Byzantine bishop of Caesarea, who wrote the first widely used Monastic Rule. Rejecting the extreme practices of the Desert Fathers, Basil opted for a more measured form of discipline, encoded in a rule of life that was "strict but not severe."[12] Long before psychologists were studying habits, he grasped the wisdom of starting small. "Don't, then, immediately try to force an overstrict discipline on yourself," he wrote. "It's better to advance in godliness little by little."[13]

That's still good advice 1,700 years later. Advance in godliness little by little.

Just crack open your Bible every day. You might only read a few verses. Or perhaps you'll slip into a groove and read several chapters. Spend a few minutes in prayer. At first, it might feel like your prayers bounce off the ceiling. But keep showing up. Just a little each day. That adds up over time. Slowly, you'll feel yourself changing. Growing closer to God. It starts small but adds up to a life of intimacy with your Creator.

REFLECT

Do you find yourself struggling to pray and read your Bible consistently? If so, what prevents you from engaging in these spiritual disciplines?

What role do emotions play? Do you have a hard time engaging in spiritual disciplines when you're not feeling particularly spiritual? What happens when you push through and do it anyway?

How can being too ambitious in your goals sabotage success? What are the benefits of starting small, even when it comes to communing with God?

Chapter Seven

Show Up for Church

Even If You're Late

I lose my cool most Sundays.

Ironically it happens while trying to get my kids ready for church. Here's a sample of the kind of things I find myself saying on a typical Sunday morning:

"The socks go on your feet, not your ears."

"Please stop hitting your sister with the lightsaber."

"Cool. You dumped yogurt on your dress."

"No, you cannot wear your Frozen costume to church."

"Stop riding the cat."

"What did I say about pouring orange juice into the toaster?"

"Why are you biting me?"

Coaxing little human beings through the delicate ballet of eating breakfast, brushing teeth, and combing hair—then getting their butts in the car—is no small undertaking. The struggle, as they say, is real.

Before having kids, going to church was easy. Grace and I could sleep in and still have enough time to hit Starbucks before the first song. Even being late wasn't so bad. We'd glide in like ninjas and grab a seat near the back.

But with three kids, our stealthy days are over. We're loud and stumbly. If we come in late, I flash a weak smile at my fellow parishioners as I guide our gaggle to a pew. Fortunately, our church is super relaxed, and no one seems to mind. At least we made it.

WHY CHURCH?

Why do we bother? It's a question a lot of people are asking these days. Fewer and fewer Americans are attending church. And, even among those who do, attendance is falling. A generation ago, many church members showed up for services each week. Today, most attend once or twice a month. In the wake of the pandemic, those numbers are slipping even lower.[1] There are a lot of things driving this trend—from secularization to Sunday soccer—but the outcome is that more and more people are staying home.

This is where you might expect me to cross my arms and scold you into faithful church attendance. *Stop slapping the snooze, you heathen! Let's get those numbers up, Christian soldier!* But I won't. I just don't have it in me. Truth is, I get it. Showing up for church is hard. And there are a lot of things that keep us from coming. Just think of all the obstacles.

You have to get up early. If you're not a morning person (and I'm not!), it means giving up one of those precious opportunities to sleep in on the weekend. There's a reason "Bedside Baptist" is the biggest church in the world. It's cozy, comfy. The pews are literally pillows! Even if you opt for an evening service, going to church is still a sacrifice. One less free evening in the week.

You also have to get ready! These days most churchgoers don't don suits and dresses. But it still requires looking semi-presentable. Like, brush your teeth. Run a comb through your hair. Get some coffee in your system. Not a herculean feat, but it's harder than lounging on the couch in sweatpants, something we all grew quite comfortable doing during the pandemic.

Going to church also means dealing with people. And people are the worst. (Please don't quote me on that.) Overly eager greeters. Close talkers. Bad singers. Noisy teens. Grumpy seniors. Rambunctious children. People who want . . . help. Even the nice people can be annoying, especially in the morning. And if it's a good church, people will get up in your business. They'll want to know how you've been, if you're struggling with anything, what you're doing after the service. They'll try to get involved in your life and show you love. Like I said, people are the worst.

These aren't even the biggest obstacles. Some people have had awful church experiences that makes going back almost impossible. Maybe they've endured a bitter church conflict or felt betrayed by their Christian community. Perhaps they've even been abused. These tragic experiences raise barriers that make going to church daunting. There are no easy answers or simple ways to get past them. And yet, with all the challenges—from the silly to the serious—I'm convinced that going to church is crucial.

"ISOLATION IS A LIAR"

I was curious about why other people go to church, so I put the question to some friends.

Why is going to church important?[2]

One person replied: "These bulletins aren't going to read themselves, you know." Fortunately, there were some serious responses too. Many emphasized the important role of community. "Isolation tells you being alone is safer," said Glenna Marshall. "But isolation is a liar. God knew we would need others so He gave us the church."

Amber Benson echoed this point. "When you want community least is when you need it most." That fits with what I've seen. I can think of many Christians who made awful decisions that blew up their lives. In most instances, it occurred in a season of isolation. They had withdrawn from their church community before making these tragic choices. I'm sure they thought they didn't need Christian friends, that they were fine on their own, but they weren't. Like Glenna said, "Isolation is a liar."

The people who responded to my question didn't view church through rose-colored lenses. They readily acknowledged the challenges presented by being part of a community of imperfect people. But they believed it was worth it anyway.

Dave Gipson wrote, "Anyone can worship alone in the woods. But you really have to love God to put up with the broken, wandering people who show up to worship with you on a Sunday."[3] It's a great point that cuts both ways. At church, you must put up with other people. But they have to put up with the broken, wandering person known as you. As Augustine said, "Put up with it, because perhaps you have been put up with."[4]

That experience of living the Christian life together is different than going it alone. As Jake Schlegel responded, "There's something uniquely transcendent about experiencing and listening to and witnessing the Holy Spirit within a community of people who you've grieved with and rejoiced with, doubted with, laughed with."

Bible teacher Beth Moore responded to my question with just one word: "Incarnation." I had to think about that one for a second before I realized she was right. When you consider that God showed up (in the flesh!) for us, it makes sense that we would show up for each other.

When you consider that God showed up (in the flesh!) for us, it makes sense that we would show up for each other.

"I'M GLAD YOU'RE HERE"

There's no doubt that you benefit immensely by being part of a church. But even when you don't feel that acute need, you should still show up. Why? Because people need you!

Some come to church brimming with joy. Their lives are going great and they're thankful and eager to worship God. But not everyone. Some barely crawled out of bed. Some of those in attendance are depressed or plagued by doubt. Others are fighting to keep their marriage from imploding or reeling from a grim diagnosis. Some aren't even sure whether God is real, and they came because somebody practically dragged them.

That was the case for the country singer Walker Hayes, known for hit songs such as "Fancy Like." After spending a decade in Nashville trying to launch a music career, and not experiencing much success, he was discouraged and drinking heavily.

Then one day his wife accepted an invite from a friend to come to church. Walker was less than enthused. "Church . . . I hated the word," he writes, "I hated how it made me feel. The word triggered guilt, shame, anger, and hurt."[5] He agreed to go but his wife had to drive. By the time the evening service rolled around, he was drunk.

They walked in late, and Hayes remembers being unimpressed with the subpar music. "It was just a white dude with an acoustic guitar in a golf hat."[6] But during the greeting time, a man named Craig Cooper approached him, and said something simple that changed his life. Walker recalls that Craig "looked me dead in the eyes knowing I was drunk, knowing I was not a believer, knowing I was as uncomfortable in those creaky old wooden pews as I was in my own skin, knowing I thought his beliefs were as crazy as believing in Santa Claus, and said, 'I'm glad you're here.'"[7]

It was a simple greeting, but it impacted Hayes deeply. "He meant it. And by the grace of God, for the first time in my life, I believed it."[8]

Walker is now a passionate believer. He and Craig are best friends. They even wrote a book together, with a title taken from that first meeting: *Glad You're Here*. Today, if you attend one of Hayes's sold-out concerts, you'll be treated to country music and stories about how Jesus changed his life.

I hate to think of how things might have been different if Craig hadn't shown up that Sunday. If there hadn't been someone willing to cut through the awkwardness to greet a stranger, to ignore the booze on his breath, and welcome him warmly.

People like Walker are sitting in churches every Sunday. They may not even want to be there. But they need help. They need someone like Craig to help them take that first step toward God.

It's not just people in a crisis that need help. Who are we kidding? We all do. Everyone who walks through the doors of a church is making an implicit admission that they're not okay on their own. It's like attending an AA meeting. You're confessing that you have problems, that you're broken, in need of grace and healing.

I remember hearing a pastor open a service by extending an unusual invitation. "Maybe you're here but are too weak to worship. That's okay. If you're in that place, you don't have to do anything. We'll worship for you. We'll pray on your behalf. Let the body of Christ carry you for a while."

How beautiful. That's how the body works. Sometimes you carry others. Sometimes they carry you.

Hebrews warns us to "not [give] up meeting together, as some are in the habit of doing" (Heb. 10:25). I've heard this verse invoked many times as a sort of legalistic requirement for church attendance, but there's a clear purpose behind the command. It's revealed in the words preceding it ("And let us consider how we may spur one another on toward love and good deeds")—and in the words after it: "but encouraging one another."

Earlier I said people are the worst. But they're the best too.

This is no arbitrary requirement. The reason we gather with fellow believers is for our mutual benefit. We need each other. Earlier I said people are the worst. But they're the best too. I get a little emotional when I think of all the ways that we've been blessed and supported by God's people over the years. The words of encouragement, the meals when we've been sick, the joking around, the friendship, the fellowship. Nothing on earth compares.

There's a whole body of research demonstrating the positive impact of church attendance. People who go to church have less depression, lower blood pressure, more stable and satisfying marriages, deeper friendships, and live up to seven years longer. They're more generous with their time and money, have better mental health, more satisfying sex lives, and even recover more quickly from surgery.[9] The benefits apply to kids as well. For adolescents, church attendance significantly decreases the "Big 3" dangers of depression, substance abuse, and sexual promiscuity.[10]

But studies can't tease out the deepest reasons for going to church. They involve more than ancillary benefits to our physical and psychological health. Going to church is about being part of Christ's body, about meshing our lives with brothers and sisters in a community that gathers to worship God and participate in His mission on earth. It's a mystical undertaking whereby we trade the comforts and convenience of individualism for membership in a spiritual collective that stretches back in history and out forever into the future.

"THE MINISTRY OF ATTENDANCE"

I recently saw an episode of *The Simpsons* where Homer dies after choking on a piece of broccoli (and here I thought the donuts would kill him).[11] After his death, Homer faces an even bigger problem. He didn't do enough good deeds to enter heaven. Desperate to secure his eternal fate, Homer's spirit travels back to earth to seek his wife's help.

"Marge, you gotta help me. I have to do one good deed to get into heaven."

When Marge presents a list of household chores he could do, Homer shakes his head.

"Whoa, whoa, whoa. I'm just trying to get in, I'm not running for Jesus."

I laughed. As you might expect from a secular cartoon, the theology is off. But Homer's reluctance to strive for perfection resonated. In fact, that's been a theme in this book. Perfectionism can sabotage you. Sometimes it helps to aim your sights a little lower and just do something small that gets you moving in the right direction. You're trying to grow, just a little bit each year.

In the first chapter, we looked at the power of plodding. We considered the example of William Carey and others who were able to accomplish great things by taking small, consistent steps. Then we looked at the importance of physical presence. We saw how helping people doesn't require eloquence or skill. You just have to be there. When it comes to finding God's will, we discovered how it's easy to overcomplicate things. Instead of trying to find a message in the stars, it's better to focus on your feet—and move them. Roles require a similar commitment. You don't have to be fully prepared; you just have to accept them. There's a similar dynamic when it comes to growing as a Christian. You don't have to master an exotic spiritual discipline with a Latin name; just open your Bible every day.

The same principle applies to your relationship with church. We twist ourselves into knots wondering exactly what role we should take on. Should we lead a small group? Start a ministry? Become an elder? Maybe even consider vocational ministry? Those are fine questions, but they put the cart before the horse. There's something you need to do before taking on any of these roles.

Simply be there.

Matt Smethurst is a big fan of church involvement. He's written books on the role of elders and deacons and tons of articles on the importance of church. But when he meets with new church members, he doesn't advise taking on a specific role. "I always encourage the individual joining the church not to try to do everything." What does he tell them to do? Devote themselves to what he calls "the ministry of attendance."[12]

In other words, he tells them just to show up to church. But he stresses that the simple act of coming to church is a bigger deal than many think, which is why he calls it a "ministry." He writes, "Showing up to church *is* serving others; to gather *is* to encourage. How could it be otherwise? You cannot regularly encourage those you only sporadically see."[13]

If you try to do too much right away, you can burn out. It's like the person who shows up at the gym for the first time in years and tries to run for an hour or bench two hundred pounds. What happens the next day? They can barely move! So, they stay away from the gym. Even once their muscles heal, they're reluctant to return. The first time was too painful.

Of course, there's an opposite error when it comes to exercise, one I made for years. Grace would urge me to go play basketball with the guys, but I'd refuse. "I'll be a liability on the court," I'd say. "I want to get in great shape and *then* go play ball so I can contribute." She saw right through my excuse. "That's dumb. Did you ever think that maybe the way to get in shape is to start playing now?"

Don't underestimate the power of simply showing up.

She was right, of course. It was only once I dragged my sneakers out of retirement and started showing up at the court that my fitness improved. It's the same with church. Some people might be tempted to try to do everything right away. They risk burnout. Others stay away because they think they have to be better before they come at all. But, as my wife might say, "that's dumb." It's by gathering with fellow brothers and sisters in Christ to worship God that you receive spiritual nourishment and begin to grow. Don't underestimate the power of simply showing up.

In *Rediscover Church*, Collin Hansen shares what he tells new church members.

> I make a big promise. And so far, no one has ever returned to complain that I misled them. I promise that if they show up consistently . . . and seek to care for others, they will get everything they want out of the church. That could be spiritual growth, friendships, biblical knowledge, or practical help. They will get whatever they want from the church by fulfilling just those two simple tasks.[14]

That's quite a promise. Spiritual growth, friendship, biblical knowledge, practical help—all just by showing up. It may sound like an exaggeration, but it's not. Because when you show up, other things naturally happen. You make friends. You get involved. You begin serving. You grow. But it all starts with the simple commitment to show up.

THE "SATURDAY NIGHT DECISION"

As I discussed at the beginning of this chapter, going to church is hard. I don't want to minimize the challenges of getting to a weekly service. I've felt them myself. We went through a season where our youngest made going to church miserable. She bawled every time we tried to leave her in the nursery and disrupted the service if we kept her in the sanctuary. Most of the time one of us (usually Grace) ended up having to watch her in our church's tiny entrance or chase her around outside. On many Sundays, we just decided to stay home.

I know a lot of faithful Christians who would love to be at church every week but can't. Some have chronic pain or weakened immune systems. Others work Sundays or have limited access to transportation. These are all real obstacles. No one makes it to church every time, not even the pastor.

But let's be honest. Most of us could make it a lot more. Too many times I've skipped church for some flimsy reason. Maybe I was up late or just felt a little lazy. To make the right choice consistently takes more than good intentions. If I wake up on Sunday morning and decide whether to go, most often I won't. I love what my friend Dean Inserra says about this: "Sunday morning church is a Saturday night decision!"[15] So true.

I recently saw pastor Darren Whitehead talking about the need to prioritize church amid a rush of other commitments. "Chances are you don't have time to serve in our church. The only way it's going to happen is if you *make* time. . . . We experience the deepest kind of peace when our convictions are aligned with our calendars."[16]

I never regret aligning my calendar to prioritize church. At our church, one of the elders, Eric, often gives the benediction at the end of the service. Eric has been through some brutal trials, including losing his son to cancer. But he has an infectious enthusiasm for Jesus. Before reading the benediction, he looks out over the congregation and asks the same question every time: "Are you glad you came to church this morning?" Every time I can say I answer with complete honesty, "Yes!"

It's not always easy to make it. It requires planning and

intentionality. It takes sacrifice. Aligning our convictions with our calendars isn't easy. But I never regret it.

Nor will you. The idea of an individual Christian, cut off from the community of believers, is alien to Scripture. When we disconnect from the church, we are the ones who suffer. We need each other for encouragement and accountability and support. Something powerful happens when we worship God together, something that doesn't happen when you slap the snooze and stay in bed on Sunday morning.

So, show up for church. Show up late if you have to. Show up happy or sad, thriving or barely holding on. Show up to carry others or to let them carry you. But show up. You'll be glad you did.

REFLECT

Why is going to church important? What obstacles cause you to miss? What steps would you have to take to attend church more regularly?

Amber Benson wrote, "When you want community least is when you need it most." Have you found that to be true? If so, why is that?

How have you been blessed by showing up for church? How can you help others who may be hurting?

Chapter Eight

Learn to Walk in the Rain

When Suffering Invades Your Life, Keep Moving

While I was a seminary student, I had a nervous breakdown. I know that's not the technical term for what happened, but it conveys something of the strange and debilitating effects of what occurred.

It all started with a minor physical symptom: my thumbs were twitching. Every few minutes they would jump toward my forefinger as if controlled by puppet strings. A few days later I experienced a burning sensation on my arms.

After investigating my symptoms online (big mistake!) I became convinced there was something seriously wrong. And it didn't take too much time online to pinpoint the problem. I remember walking into the office where Grace was working at the time to give her my diagnosis. My eyes were wide.

"We need to talk," I said, "I think I have MS [multiple sclerosis]."

In my mind's eye, the future was all too clear. My poor young wife would have to push me around in a wheelchair by day and hoist me into bed every night. She'd have to work doubly hard to support us both. Of course, I knew nothing about MS, including the fact that most sufferers lead active, productive lives.

The next day I entered the doctor's office barking about my MS symptoms. After a few minutes of listening to me, the doctor leaned forward and firmly said, "You do not have MS."

I didn't believe her.

After a few weeks, even I had to admit the MS diagnosis didn't quite fit. But a new, more terrifying specter rose in its place: ALS.

And so began a months-long journey of being convinced I had a degenerative neurological disease of some kind. People tried to talk sense into me, told me not to jump to conclusions, but I wasn't convinced.

The truth was, there was more than just physical symptoms. I was experiencing something that's tough to describe, even for a word nerd like me. I felt inexplicably sad. I had a constant, grinding anxiety that made concentration impossible. Forget reading or writing. I couldn't even watch TV. I had to be reminded to shave and shower. My resting heart rate was 120 beats per minute.

I tried to go back to school but could only make it a few minutes into a lecture before being overcome by a nameless dread and slipping out the back door. I ended up dropping all of my classes, which my professors were kind enough to let me wrap up later.

For a couple weeks, I'd wake up in the middle of the night overcome by a suffocating feeling that I was dying. Sometimes I'd flee our little apartment to find reprieve in the night air or just pace until the sun came up. I didn't know it at the time, but I was experiencing classic panic attacks.

I was still absolutely convinced all these symptoms were caused by an underlying physical illness. I remember explaining it with growing frustration to a different doctor. "There's something wrong with me. And it's *physiological*, not *psychological*."

I was a nightmare patient. I wouldn't accept the conclusions of medical professionals. And I had an aversion to taking medication. Those medications were for weak-minded people, not sane, strong, well-adjusted people like me!

I'd always had some psychological peculiarities. I checked my sheets every night for spiders before climbing into bed, and my shoes for hiding arachnids (I'm told this is weird). I also struggled with depression, but nothing incapacitating. Just par for the course for an aspiring writer, I told myself.

But this was different. My world had been turned upside-down. For the next year, my life returned to a level of normalcy (I'm an excellent public faker), but inwardly I was still tortured by fears and a grinding anxiety that would leave me physically exhausted by the end of each day.[1]

Up to that point, my life had been easy. Sure, I'd had the odd frustration and setback. But I'd had an idyllic childhood. I'd grown up and married the girl of my dreams. I was healthy and seemingly invincible. But suddenly that seemed to change. My days were dominated by angst and fear and uncertainty. My happy life was gone.

NO UMBRELLAS ALLOWED

We all suffer. Eventually. You might avoid it for a while. But sooner or later, it comes for you. "Man is born to trouble as surely as sparks fly upward," is how the writer of Job put it (Job 5:7). Suffering is inevitable, inescapable. It's just part of life. You can't walk through the rain without getting wet.

We trick ourselves into thinking we'll be smart enough or lucky enough to avoid serious suffering. Yet deep down we know that is no more than a comforting illusion. As author Tim Keller writes, "No matter what precautions we take, no matter how well we have put together a good life, no matter how hard we have worked to be healthy, wealthy, comfortable with friends and family, and successful with our career—something will inevitably ruin it."[2]

Cheerful stuff, eh? Sorry to be such a downer. But it's important to be real, especially about this subject. We've looked at the need to show up for different people, and in various circumstances. But this is perhaps where the mandate is most difficult—and most important.

Showing up while you're suffering.

When suffering crashes into your life, it can feel like the world stops. And maybe you wish that it would. Just for a bit so you can catch your breath. It would be nice to check out long enough to resolve the issue or at least come to terms with it. That's not how life works, of course. You can't press pause until you feel better. The responsibilities keep coming.

A few years ago, there was an ad on TV for NyQuil that always brought a smile to my face. In the commercial, a man battling a head cold pops his head into what we assume is an office. "Dave, I'm sorry to interrupt," he says. "But I've got to take a sick day tomorrow." That's when the camera spins around to show us Dave—a toddler bouncing in his crib, looking blankly at his father. The ad concludes with these words: "Dads don't take sick days. Dads take NyQuil."[3]

As a father of young kids, I understand the ad all too well. Being a parent means taking care of your kids—regardless of how lousy you feel. That's true of life in general. The world doesn't stop spinning because you're suffering. There are still bills and meetings and after-school pickups. There are still people relying on you. I'm not saying you shouldn't rest or cut back on work if you're dealing with acute suffering. But most hardship lands somewhere between annoying and incapacitating. And for most of us, checking out isn't an option. You must keep going.

The movie *Invictus* tells the true story of the relationship between Nelson Mandela (played by Morgan Freeman) and the captain of South Africa's rugby team, Francois Pienaar (played by Matt Damon). The two form an unlikely partnership to help unite their country in the wake of apartheid. In one scene of the movie, when Pienaar first meets Mandela, the president asks him about his injured ankle.

We never play at full strength. But showing up requires that we keep playing somehow anyway.

"Is it healed?" Mandela asks.

"The truth is, sir, you never really play at 100 percent, no matter what."

Mandela smiles. "Ah, yes," he responds. "In sports as in life."

We're never fully free from pain and suffering. We never play at full strength. But showing up requires that we keep playing somehow anyway.

I live twenty minutes north of Portland, Oregon. I didn't grow up in the Northwest, but I've lived here long enough to appreciate aspects of the culture, even some of the ones that "keep Portland weird." One of those things is their attitude toward rain. In the Northwest, the sky is a leaky faucet no one can fix. From September to April, it drizzles, sprinkles, or downright pours. We get a mind-boggling forty-three inches of rain per year. Transplants like me curse the gray skies, but native Northwesterners seem to embrace it. They don't hide from the rain. And, as they'll proudly tell you, they *don't* use umbrellas. One study found that 70 percent of native Northwesterners have never bought an umbrella.[4] And they don't hide out at home. They venture out on bike rides and hikes, unwilling to let a little precipitation prevent them from exploring their beautiful surroundings.

To me, it's a helpful illustration for how to deal with suffering. You can hide from suffering. You can curse it. You can painstakingly avoid every threat to your happiness and safety. You can purchase the best possible umbrella money can buy. But avoiding suffering is about as futile as avoiding rain in Oregon. And sometimes it's best just to walk in it. Even when it's really bad.

JOY AHEAD

I wish I could say my experience with anxiety and depression ended after that first awful bout in my twenties. But, like it is for many, it has been an ongoing battle. I've made a tremendous amount of progress since I had my breakdown. But my experience during seminary still runs through my life like a fault line. There's a clear before and after. Before, my brain and body were invisible to me. I didn't have to think about them. I could depend on them. They never caused any problems. But ever since that experience, it's been a struggle. My fight-or-flight instinct is easily triggered, and anxiety and depression threaten to overwhelm me, particularly in stressful seasons of life.

The worst thing we can do is battle alone. God uses people to encourage us, to inspire us to keep walking even when it rains.

The depression and anxiety are still there, but I've learned how to manage. It required being on medication for a time and learning to recognize dangerous thought patterns. And I'm blessed to have a wise and patient wife who keeps me off WebMD and snaps me out of it when I start marinating in existential angst. I've also benefited from the help of family and friends. When I first experienced anxiety and depression, my instinct was to close off from others and try to fix it myself. But these things thrive in the shadows. God put us in community for a reason. We aren't designed to navigate life on our own. That may be doubly true for those of us who struggle with depression and anxiety. The worst thing we can do is battle alone. God uses people to encourage us, to inspire us to keep walking even when it rains.

For me, one of those people was Bethany.

During the COVID lockdowns, I found myself at a low point again. Spending day after day at home isn't good for anyone's mental health, and mine was starting to crack. I was fighting anxiety—and it was starting to win. That's when I received a message from Bethany. She'd read my book about self-control and wanted to let me know about the impact it had on her life.

In the book, I told a story from the *Argonautica*, a Greek epic.

The Argonauts must sail past the sirens, the seductive but deadly mermaids. But they have a secret weapon on board: the legendary musician and poet Orpheus. When the song of the sirens reaches the ears of the sailors, Orpheus draws his lyre and plays a "sweeter song," which drowns out the voices of the mermaids and lets the sailors pass by safely. In my book, I encouraged readers to tune their ears to the sweeter song of God's purpose for their life to avoid falling prey to destructive voices.

As I discovered from Bethany's letter, her life was anything but easy. And after I finished reading it, I wondered if she should be the one writing the books instead of me. Here's what she wrote to me:

> *I have been dealing with mysterious and severe chronic illnesses since 2015. It all came to a head in April 2019 when I was seen at the Cleveland Clinic for centralized pain and random spells that left my arms and legs paralyzed. I saw one of the world's foremost neurologists who diagnosed me with a rare disease and a treatment plan that completely upended my life. I needed to completely rewire my brain to encounter stimuli and not go into paralysis.*

The letter explained how she was disappointed to learn that there wasn't a pill or surgery to fix the problem. The regimen the doctor prescribed was demanding. She confessed she implemented it half-heartedly initially, and the paralysis and pain returned.

She continued:

> *I read your book in January and it revolutionized my life. The phrase "Listen to the Sweeter Song" held me to what the doctor*

said. I wanted to get better; I knew if I obeyed the doctor I would. We fasted and prayed for YEARS for an answer and now that it was here, I didn't like it. But I could show self-control and listen to the sweeter song of obedience. . . .

I was no longer following the instructions "to get better" but doing it out of obedience for what God called me to do. I continued working hard and keeping up with my regimen. This past fall was some of the BEST I have felt in years! . . .

In November 2020, one of my physical therapists got me sick with COVID. It's been a painful 38 days dealing with long-haul COVID. I've really only been out of bed for eight of them? In some ways, I've regressed. . . .

I had told my physical therapist about "listen to the sweeter song" back in January and how it helped me to pull through difficult moments when I just wanted to quit. Last week I was on her table, broken physically and emotionally. She looked at me and said, "Bethany—I think you need to listen to the sweeter song again."

I'm still couch-and-bed bound. But I know God is calling me back toward obedience. COVID is the hardest illness I have faced. . . . But God is good. I have a path forward to take. And I'm going to sing along to the sweeter song as I go.[5]

As I read Bethany's message, tears filled my eyes. She had written to tell me about how my book had helped her, but she was the one ministering to me. I was moved by her stubborn obedience, the commitment to keep moving forward in the face of tremendous obstacles and setbacks. Suffering is not a competitive sport, but I couldn't help feeling slightly ashamed. I'd been marinating in self-pity over challenges that were minor compared to the ones she faced. Her letter served as a gentle rebuke. She had faced death but came out hopeful, determined. As she wrote, "But God is good. I have a path forward to take." If she could keep going, so could I.

In his book *Beautiful People Don't Just Happen*, my friend Scott Sauls shares story after story of people who have endured life's storms and emerged better on the other side. He describes a mother who lost her teenaged son to suicide, a thirty-five-year-old man with terminal cancer, a songwriter who lost his eyesight. He borrowed the title for his book from grief expert Elisabeth Kübler-Ross, who observed:

> The most beautiful people we have known are those who have known defeat, known suffering, known struggle, known loss, and have found their way out of the depths. These persons have an appreciation, a sensitivity, and an understanding of life that fills them with compassion, gentleness, and a deep loving concern. Beautiful people do not just happen.[6]

As Sauls points out, suffering doesn't automatically result in beauty. But if we walk with God through our pain, He uses it to transform us into who He wants us to be.

The greatest example of faithfulness in the face of suffering came from Jesus. It's hard to imagine a more painful plight than the one Christ endured. He was betrayed by His closest friends, beaten, mocked, and nailed to a cross. Perhaps most painful of all, He suffered the silence of His Father. It's worth noting that Jesus didn't float serenely toward that dreadful day. He sweat "drops of blood" as He prayed on the eve of His crucifixion (Luke 22:44). But He didn't run. He had His sights set on what would come after. The writer of Hebrews tells us that He endured the cross "for the joy set before him" (Heb. 12:2). He knew that His pain wasn't the final chapter, that God was using it and that there was "joy set before him."

I want to encourage you to do the same. If you're in a season of suffering, this isn't the end. As the famous line, often attributed to Winston Churchill, goes, "If you're going through hell, keep going." As Christians, we know suffering doesn't have the final word. There is joy set before you. There is hope. So be like Bethany and keep moving forward. Toss your umbrella and walk in the rain. Remember what my friend Scott Sauls says. Beautiful people don't just happen. You're becoming one of those beautiful people right now. Just keep going.

REFLECT

What is your immediate reaction when you suffer? How does it change the way you relate to the people around you? How does it change the way you relate to God?

How does having a lot of responsibilities complicate things when you deal with hardship? In those times, how can you show up for yourself and get the rest and help you need? How can you continue showing up for others, despite the challenges you face?

When you're going through hardship, is it difficult to see the joy ahead? Does it help to remember that God may be working through the experience to make you a more beautiful person?

Chapter Nine

Practice Incarnation

You Don't Need to Be Perfect, Just Present

It was like a movie scene when the main character hits a breaking point and does something totally unexpected. But William Cimillo was a real person, and his workaday existence was anything but dramatic.

Maybe that's why he snapped.

The year was 1947, and Cimillo was a bus driver in New York City. He was sick of his job.

"I was on the job for about 20 years and I really got tired of it all. Up and down every day, the same people, the same stops, nickels, dimes, transfers."[1]

Then one day, he'd finally had enough.

"Instead of making a right turn to go off to my route, I thought I'd make a left turn," he recalled.[2]

That left turn turned into quite a road trip. Instead of picking up passengers in the Bronx, Cimillo crossed the Washington Bridge.

"It was a beautiful morning. The sun was shining," Cimillo remembers. After stopping in Jersey for breakfast, he got back behind the wheel of the bus and kept driving. "Before I knew it. . . . I was right in front of the White House."[3]

He kept moving. Heading south, he picked up a hitchhiker (there was plenty of room) who rode with him for a couple of days in the cavernous city bus. Finally, Cimillo reached Hollywood, Florida, just north of Miami. He went for a late-night dip in the ocean. "Moonlight bathing," Cimillo called it. "I enjoyed that very much."[4]

The next day he hit the racetracks. He was 1,300 miles away from the noisy traffic of New York City. But his joyride had a problem: he was running out of money. He telegraphed his boss a request for $50, claiming the bus had broken down. Instead of sending money, his boss called the authorities. Two police officers showed up and arrested Cimillo.

You'd think that's where the story would end. Cimillo would return home, lose his job, and face criminal charges. Instead, when Cimillo was led off the bus in handcuffs in front of the police department in Manhattan, he was greeted by a crowd of hundreds of cheering fans. Word had gotten out about the renegade bus driver. He had become a local folk hero and a national news story.

An NBC newscaster effused, "William Cimillo. The busman who took a holiday. And brother, what a holiday. Just wanted to drive, feel the tang of spring in the air. Busmen in the Bronx greeted their passengers today with a cry, all aboard for Florida!"[5]

The *New York World-Telegram* described why so many found Cimillo's actions relatable. "We know just how he felt. Who hasn't yearned for escape, for change, for fairer scenes?"[6]

The charges against Cimillo were serious. He was indicted on charges of grand larceny and faced up to ten years in prison. But the court of public opinion would have the final say. Cimillo's colleagues organized a fundraising drive to cover his legal fees, and eventually the Department of Transportation decided to drop the charges. Cimillo was even given his job back. On his first day back on his route, people lined up to squeeze onto his bus. A crowd of hundreds of screaming high school girls clamored for his autograph.

For the rest of his life, Cimillo was a hero.

A SCARED YOUNG BOY

I heard Cimillo's story on a radio show and it brought a smile to my face. Who hasn't been stuck in a monotonous job and dreamed about breaking free in radical fashion? For most of us that's where the impulse stays—in our dreams. But Cimillo actually did it. He turned left instead of right and went on a grand adventure.

But the radio show wasn't over. In addition to telling the story of Cimillo's famous joyride, they interviewed his oldest son, Richard. He remembers his father's sudden fame. "He just felt like a star, I guess. He was recognized wherever he went. . . . every time we went out, every place we went, there was always—you know, it was like a movie star."[7]

But the novelty wore on the rest of the family. "After a while, I think my mother got tired of it. And I got tired of it. You know what I'm saying? But he never got tired of it."[8]

Richard's lack of enthusiasm made sense when I heard of how his father's impromptu flight from reality unfolded from his perspective.

"Let me explain something to you. I was 12 years old at the time. And after I come home from school, my mother was crying. And I was, well, Ma, why are you crying? And she said, well, he didn't come home. I wonder where he is. Why wouldn't he come home for supper, and all that. And next day, the same thing. He didn't come home. Not a phone call."[9]

Richard feared his father's bus had been in a horrible accident. He believed his dad was dead. Even after they found out what happened, he was haunted by the fact that his dad didn't let them know earlier.

"I don't know if my mother ever asked, why didn't you call. I never asked. He never called. Not a word. You know, I looked up to him, he was my father. But after the Florida incident, I had problems. I had problems looking up. That was a tough time for me."

Richard's story complicated the narrative for me. When Cimillo took his spontaneous trip, he wasn't just abandoning his route; he was hurting his family. To thousands of New Yorkers, he was a hero. But one scared boy saw things differently.

A TALE OF TWO DADS

We live in a world that glamorizes the leavers: people who shake off the expectations of others to pursue their dreams at all costs. Sometimes, it's good to be a renegade—but often we forget the collateral damage such actions leave in their wake. Perhaps nowhere is this truer than when it comes to parenting.

I remember having conversations with two friends about their fathers. Neither father was perfect. What father is? But I thought there were interesting similarities—and profound differences.

Chase (not his real name) had a dad who had been in and out of his life since the beginning. More out than in. He would drop by to see Chase on the odd birthday or holiday. He'd call once in a while. When Chase got a little older, something changed. "Dad got really religious," Chase explained. He would visit and gush about his newfound faith in God. Unfortunately, his involvement in his son's life was still sporadic. And when he did come by, it was often to ask for money and preach at his now-grown son. "It gets a little old," Chase confessed. "He tells us everything that we're doing wrong. After a while I just have to tell him, 'Okay, that's enough.'"

Given his father's shortcomings, Chase remains remarkably kind about his dad. "It's all good," he said. "He's got his problems but that's okay." Chase's wife on the other hand, is less sanguine. "He's a weird guy," she told me.

A few months after my conversation with Chase, I talked to my friend Marshall Allen about his dad. Marshall's dad was the quiet type. Really quiet. "He didn't have a lot to say," Marshall said. "Sometimes he would sit there through a whole meal with the family and hardly say a word."

I was perplexed. Raised in a hyper-social family with a gregarious dad, I couldn't imagine the scenario. "Was he angry?" I asked. "Oh, not at all," Marshall said. "He was just extremely quiet."

Having a taciturn father made for a unique experience for the young Marshall. "I never had 'the talk' with my dad," Marshall said. "We never had a man-to-man talk at all really."

But Marshall's dad spoke in other ways. Marshall recalls seeing him up at 5:00 a.m. every morning, sitting in his armchair, with the Bible splayed open across his lap. He also made a point of attending all his sons' sporting events. "He never missed a game," Marshall recalls. "I knew he loved me, even though he almost never said it."

Marshall's dad, Darrell Allen, recently passed away after a battle with dementia. Marshall is an award-winning journalist, and he wrote a column paying tribute to his father. He described him as "a man of few words," who nevertheless devoted his entire life to serving God and loving his family.[10]

"Dad never talked to me about being a faithful husband. He demonstrated it," Marshall wrote. "I never saw him argue with my mom or put her down. I never saw him put himself first. I watched him serve her. Mom's been afflicted by a lot of health issues . . . through it all, Dad cared for her selflessly."

It was the same story when it came to parenting. "Dad did not tell me how to be a good father," Marshall added. But in addition to attending every sporting event of his children, Marshall wrote that "it was always clear that his family came before his career. . . . He turned down opportunities that would require him to travel more or work long hours. He wanted to be there for our family.

"My dad was 'old school' all the way. He grew up in a farming family and was the first in his family to get a college degree. He wasn't affectionate or expressive with his love, but we never doubted his love or loyalty to us."

It was a powerful tribute to a truly remarkable and faithful man. Sure, Marshall's dad could have been more verbally affirming. But when I ask myself which father was better—Chase's or Marshall's—there's no question about the answer. Marshall's dad wins by a mile. Why? He wasn't perfect, but he was present. Perhaps he could have said more, but he was there. He showed up. And his godly example and steady presence set a pattern for his children's lives and let them know they were loved.

"SAME CHEESE AND MACARONI"

What do these stories of Cimillo, Chase, and Marshall show us?

Presence matters.

I find this truth tremendously reassuring. I'm in the thick of parenting right now, and once in a while I'm seized by a fear that I'm messing up. Parenting is a head trip. It's not just the actual challenges of raising kids that are tough. It's the thousand competing theories about how to parent properly that clamor for my attention.

Should you let your baby "cry it out" at night or opt for attachment parenting and let them sleep in your bed? As they grow, should they spend the bulk of their days in free play to nurture their imaginations? Or should you push them to read and write as early as possible? Should you take every possible precaution to keep them safe—or opt for "free range" parenting to help build resilience?

There are noisy experts on each side of these debates, all claiming your child's future hangs in the balance. Am I choosing the right approach to each of these issues? I'm not sure. Then there are things that I know I'm doing wrong, like giving them too much sugar and screen time. We're constantly trying to rein in both, but it's a battle.

I also worry that I'm doing a poor job of teaching them the faith. A while back I overheard our two oldest kids in a strange argument over who was better, God or Jesus. My son insisted Jesus has the edge because He walked on water. My daughter shot back that God is better because He is Jesus' boss. I chuckled at the silly exchange, but it got me wondering about how well I am teaching them the basics of Christian beliefs.

I also worry whether I'm modeling the kind of faith that they will find compelling. Am I giving them a foundation in the faith that will withstand the storms of adolescence and early adulthood? I hope so, but I'm not completely confident. I wonder if I'm messing up in that department too.

There are no perfect parents. But I take comfort in the fact that I'm succeeding in at least one area: being there.

Actually, I don't wonder if I'm messing up; I know I am. At least to some degree. We all are. There are no perfect parents. But I take comfort in the fact that I'm succeeding in at least one area: being there. The Bible says that "love covers over a multitude of sins" (1 Peter 4:8). I believe that applies to parenting. My kids don't have to wonder where I am or if I'm going to leave. And my presence says I love them.

I was reflecting on the crucial role of present-yet-imperfect fathers last Father's Day. I took to Twitter to give a tongue-in-cheek kudos to all "the mediocre dads who are still showing up." While timelines were brimming with stories about the best dads in the world, I wanted to encourage the ones who were showing up despite their shortcomings. "Your presence provides a baseline of psychological security that will pay dividends throughout your kid's life," I wrote.

My friend Christine Fain agreed, restating the point in frank terms.

"Mostly, children can handle anything as long as there's some stability. Same person, same house, same cheese and macaroni."[11]

It was a point reiterated by parenting experts Daniel J. Siegel and Tina Payne Bryson in their book *The Power of Showing Up*: "You don't have to be perfect; you can't be. . . . They [your children] don't need every advantage, and they don't need a superparent. They just need you—authentic, flawed, and fully present you."[12]

We can all grow and become better parents. But the most fundamental gift we provide our children is our presence.

IT'S ALL QUALITY TIME

We hear a lot about the importance of quality time, giving our children our undivided attention. It's an area I know I can improve in. When I'm with my kids, it's easy to check out and look at my phone. I remember being glued to my phone as my son tried to tell me about something that happened at school. Finally, he reached over and pulled my phone away from my face. When I snapped at him, his shoulders slumped. "I just wanted your attention," he said. Not exactly my proudest parenting moment.

It's easy to forget how much kids crave your undivided attention. About the best thing I can do for my son (more than gifts or candy or parties) is to set my phone down and say, "Tell me about dinosaurs."

That's a challenge as a parent because often we're not into the same things that our kids are. They're at a different developmental stage, and their interests don't match ours. I don't really care about dinosaur facts (though I have learned some fascinating ones from my son). I'm perfectly indifferent to Disney princesses. But I do care about my kids, and for that reason, I should try to enter their world.

Being present with your children also takes patience. Recently,

I went for a walk to pick up the mail (our neighborhood has shared mailboxes, so it's a few blocks away). It was a lovely, warm day so I brought my youngest along. I figured it would be a quick stroll.

It wasn't.

Halfway there my daughter decided it was time for a break. She ambled onto a neighbor's lawn, sat down, and buried her tiny fingers in the lush, green grass. I let her sit there for a minute or two, but impatience got the best of me. "Okay, honey," clapping my hands, "let's get going."

After coaxing her back to the sidewalk we resumed our journey, but she walked slowly, running a hand along each parked car we passed. "No, no, those aren't our cars. Don't touch them." When she stooped to examine a car tire, I'd had enough. I snatched her up into my arms and carried her to the mailbox.

The walk back was even slower. She spotted a patch of aging dandelions and stopped to pick them. She paused to admire each one before blowing their white, fuzzy seeds into the breeze. "Let's go!" I pleaded. "Mom's waiting for us."

When we finally made it back to the house, I could feel my blood pressure rising. I was annoyed. But why?

It was a Saturday and I had nothing to do. The weather was nice. But somehow having a five-minute walk stretch into twenty minutes was too much for me. I had an objective for that walk: get the mail and get back. My child's meandering changed the plan, and I couldn't handle it. I should have meandered with her. I should have squatted down and felt the grass and picked dandelions. I should have been present. It's crucial to slow down and give your children your full attention, to have that quality time.

Recently, I posed a question online. It was for parents of

grown children: "How much would you pay to go back and hold your kids when they were small?"[13]

I wasn't ready for the deluge of replies, many peppered with crying emojis. "Everything I have," one lady wrote. "My oldest will be eighteen this week, heading to college in the fall, and I just want to hold her in a rocking chair one more time."

Even on days when I'm exhausted by the demands of fatherhood, it helps to remember that I'm in a phase of life that many would give anything to revisit.

The other replies were just as dramatic.

"Anything," "A bajillion dollars," "All the money I have plus coffee," "Why are you trying to make me cry?"

I know a lot of the responses were tongue-in-cheek, but it underscored just how precious those years are. It was an excellent reminder for me not to squander the time I have with my children. Even on days when I'm exhausted by the demands of fatherhood, it helps to remember that I'm in a phase of life that many would give anything to revisit. When I realize how quickly this time passes, I'm less likely to be distracted or disengaged.

Yet as important as quality time is, it's no replacement for *quantity* time—just spending lots of time together. You can't offset working eighty hours a week by giving your kids sixty minutes of attention on a Saturday afternoon. You can't compensate for your absence with Xboxes and *Frozen*-themed parties. When it comes to parenting, there's no substitute for just being there, day in and day out.

It's in that quantity time that most of life happens. You walk to get the mail. You clean the house. You peel potatoes. You fight. You make up. You drive each other crazy. You laugh and cry, eat and sleep. And it all matters. They're learning, growing. With you. It's all quality time.

I realize not every family situation is idyllic. Divorce makes being there all the time impossible. So do many jobs that require you to leave for weeks at a time. Whatever the challenges, though, we can all strive to spend more time with our children. We can be there as much as possible, knowing that the eighteen years they spend in our care are so crucial—time we'll never get back.

NOT JUST FOR PARENTS

I also realize that not everyone has children. But the principle of presence applies beyond the home.

Before we had kids, I signed up to mentor two twelve-year-old boys. They both had family situations that were less than ideal, and I was excited about the chance to make a difference in their lives. My initial enthusiasm waned, however, after our first outing together. I could barely get them to look at me, let alone talk. My questions about school and sports were met with one-word answers, and I wondered if I was cut out for mentoring.

Finally, after a few times out together, I found a topic that got them excited: video games. Unfortunately, it was a topic I knew little about. I had played *Mario Bros.* and *Duck Hunt* as a kid, a fact that didn't seem to impress them. I had envisioned them opening up to me, sharing their dreams and confiding in me about their struggles, but there was none of that. Mostly, it was just us driving around or going out to eat, the awkward silence broken only by talk of video games. I wondered if our weekly meetings were even worth it.

But one time as I dropped off one of the boys, he asked if I was coming back next week. "Yeah, of course!" I said. "Good," he said, and smiled. Suddenly, I saw it. He liked hanging out, looked forward to it, even. His dad wasn't involved in his life and the presence of this stranger, who had no idea how to relate to twelve-year-olds and zero knowledge of video games, was somehow appreciated. My presence was making a difference.

Be a mentor, a friend. You don't have to be cool, just care. No need to be perfect, just present.

As I found out, it doesn't take much to make an impact.

I've talked to a lot of older Christians distraught at the number of young people leaving the faith. Many of them seem to be waiting for someone else to reverse the trend. They think maybe their church needs to hire cooler pastors or invest in a smoke machine for the sanctuary. But perhaps the biggest predictor of whether young people will retain their faith is whether they have intergenerational relationships with people in the church.[14] In other words, if they have connections with older believers. I always tell these concerned older Christians that they may be the answers to their own prayers. If you take an interest in a younger person in your church, it will do wonders. Take them out for lunch, ask them about their lives. Be a mentor, a friend. You don't have to be cool, just care. No need to be perfect, just present.

When they close the casket on you, no one will talk about your dazzling performance at the office. No one will care about what you drove. No one will remember what you posted on Instagram. But they will remember your presence. They will recall you picking them up from school or sitting in the stands at their soccer game. They will remember you praying with them or dropping off a meal when they were sick. They will feel your arm on their shoulder when they needed support. They will remember that, imperfect though you were, you were there. They will remember that you showed up.

REFLECT

Think back to your childhood. Who made the greatest impact on you? How did they do it?

Is it reassuring to hear the difference just being present makes? How can you organize your schedule to be more present for your family?

Are there ways you can show up for people outside your family?

Chapter Ten

Let Something Slide

Because You Can't Show Up for Everything

I've come to a sad realization. I'll probably never have a nice yard.

Our yard is brown, patchy. It's the kind of yard where kids park bikes and dig for worms. When it rains, it gets a little greener, but if you look closely, you'll notice there's more crabgrass than real grass—and a lot of weeds. In the summer it's an abomination. The grass turns a sickly yellow and blotches of dirt appear. I like to brag that we have the most environmentally friendly lawn in the neighborhood.

At one point we resolved to do something about it. I had visions of the lawns you see in TV commercials. You know the ones. The kind where lemonade is served. Where children play in sprinklers and a golden retriever runs in slow motion on a carpet of lush, green grass.

So, we sprinkled seed. We watered. We fertilized. A few weeks later fresh shoots peeked through the soil, but there were too few of them. Eventually they were overwhelmed by weeds and crabgrass, and the yard returned to its desolate state.

We went to Home Depot and sought out someone wearing an orange vest. What should we do? "Don't bother," was the reply. "The soil around here is like clay. Nothing grows." Apparently, laying sod was the only surefire solution. And that wasn't in the budget.

Even with sod, I knew maintaining a nice lawn wouldn't be easy. It would require weeding, fertilizing, mowing, spraying, and probably other stuff I didn't even know about. It would mean that every time the neighbor kids ran across the grass, I'd need to summon my inner grumpy old man and shout, "GET OFF MY LAWN!"

The biggest issue though? I'm busy. I have a young family and a demanding career. Having a perfect yard isn't high enough on my list of priorities. And that's okay.

Which brings me to the point of my sad-yard confession. It's simply this.

You gotta let something slide.

THE BEAUTY OF BOUNDARIES

Let something slide. It sounds bad, I know. You might be feeling a little whiplash right now. After all, we have explored the necessity of doing important things like showing up for people, reading your Bible, attending church, and being there for your family. But the fact that we have important things to do underscores the necessity of not doing everything. Letting something slide enables you to show up for the things that truly matter.

We think we can do it all. And do it all well! This is the year you're going to kill it at work, eat healthy, read with your kids every night, get washboard abs, cook gourmet meals, host parties, get more involved at church, organize your garage, remodel the bathroom, and chair the PTA. Oh, and you're finally going to take all those unused vacation days too.

Feels kind of silly when you see it all written down, doesn't it? As the old Yiddish saying goes, "Man plans, God laughs."

Yet many of us still believe that, somehow, we really can do it all. If you're still suffering from such delusions, let me be blunt. You won't because you can't. Even if you fine-tune your time management and employ the best life hacks and read the right books (including this one), you still won't get everything done. And rather than beating yourself up about that fact, it's best to make peace with it.

The truth underlying this reality can be captured in one word: *finitude*. Our finitude impacts everything. Our time is limited. Our energy is limited. Our resources are limited. Even our willpower is limited.

A few years ago, I saw a friend touting some unusual wall art on social media. He'd hung a "My Life in Weeks" poster up in his office. It was a calendar of sorts, breaking down a ninety-year life into tiny squares. Each square represented one week, with the ones he'd already lived shaded black. It was a stark reminder of the brevity of life—and that was the point. Even if you live to ninety (which is well beyond the average lifespan) seeing your life reduced to a series of little squares is sobering. I wasn't quite cozy enough with my own mortality to order one for my wall, but I understand why it works. "Slightly terrifying. Extremely effective," is how one website selling the posters describes it.[1]

It was the same idea behind the popular time management book *Four Thousand Weeks*. The book's title is a reference to the approximate number of weeks a person lives. It begins with this stark assessment: "The average human lifespan is absurdly, insultingly brief."[2] Yet instead of creating fear, the author argues that glimpsing the brevity of life offers freedom.

"But that isn't a reason for unremitting despair, or for living in an anxiety-fueled panic about making the most of your limited time. It's a cause for relief. You get to give up on something that was always impossible—the quest to become the optimized, infinitely capable, emotionally invincible, fully independent person you're officially supposed to be. Then you get to roll up your sleeves and start work on what's gloriously possible instead."[3]

God never demanded we be infinite. He only calls us to be faithful.

Of all people, Christians should be most accepting of our finitude. We know, as Scripture reminds us, that we are "dust" (Ps. 103:14), "a mist that appears for a little while and then vanishes" (James 4:14). Furthermore, the Bible links accepting the brevity of life to wisdom: "Teach us to number our days, that we may gain a heart of wisdom" (Ps. 90:12).

Yet, as theologian Kelly M. Kapic writes, "Christians often confuse finitude and sin." In other words, we think that not being able to accomplish everything is some sort of moral failing. As a result, "we feel guilty about things we shouldn't feel guilty about." Rather than wallowing in guilt, Kapic believes we should celebrate when we crash into our limitations. When we embrace our limitations, "We begin to relate to God and others in a more fruitful way: no longer do we aspire to have infinite capacity—that is God's job! . . . We do not apologize for our creaturely needs and dependence on others, for we discover this is how God made us, and it is good."[4]

Kapic is right. God never demanded we be infinite. He only calls us to be faithful.

Do you struggle with accepting your limitations? I do. Of course, I'll own up to the obvious fact that I'm a finite creature with limited capacity. But in practice, it's a different matter. I have a hard time turning down requests and invitations and just admitting I don't have the bandwidth to pull it off.

But when I do opt out of things, what a relief! And, surprisingly, I find most people understand. In fact, studies have found that telling people no is not as costly as people expect. Summarizing the findings of eleven studies on the topic, organizational psychologist Adam Grant writes, "People overestimate the relationship and reputation risks of turning down requests. People generally don't hold it against you."[5]

In other words, they cut you some slack. And you should cut yourself some slack too. There's liberty in acknowledging your limitations. Realizing you will never meet all your goals helps you shed false guilt. Ironically, it makes you more effective. Perfectionism is paralyzing. When you're trying to be the best at everything, you get frustrated and quit. Or never even start in the first place. But when you're realistic about your finitude, you're freed to work at a steady, healthy pace.

Perfectionism is paralyzing. When you're trying to be the best at everything, you get frustrated and quit.

FREE LIKE A FARMER

I had the honor of interviewing beloved author Eugene Peterson shortly before his death. At one point, Peterson, who spent most of his adult life pastoring in rural communities, said, "I never met a farmer who was in a hurry. They know there is simply too much to do."

Peterson related his observation to the calling of the pastor, but it's a good reminder for all of us. There's something about admitting you can't do it all that both slows you down and keeps you going. You realize that, as theologian Reinhold Niebuhr wrote, "Nothing that is worth doing can be achieved in your lifetime" anyway.[6] Armed with this healthy realism, you don't wear yourself out with frenetic effort. Instead, you chip away at what is "gloriously possible" with a sort of quiet determination.

One practical way I've wrestled with this reality is in how I structure my workdays. I've been working from home for almost a decade. When I first started, a friend who'd been working from home for a while let me in on a secret. "The best thing about working from home is that you can work whenever you want," he told me. "The *worst* thing about working from home is you can work whenever you want."

I soon found he was right on both counts. The flexibility was wonderful. Unfettered by the nine-to-five schedule of office life, I could take breaks when I needed to. Sometimes I'd go to the gym in the middle of the day or meet a friend for coffee. Didn't get enough sleep the night before? I could always sneak upstairs for a little nap (even though Grace wasn't thrilled when she caught me). Even frittering away large chunks of time online was easier to do without a boss peering over my shoulder. Wasting time during the day was no big deal, I told myself.

But there was a problem. Even though my schedule was more flexible, the workload was the same. Taking a morning off meant working in the evening. Too often I ended up scattering my work across a sixteen-hour window. And that took a toll on my family. On more than one occasion, Grace would fling open the door to my office in the evening, a spatula in her hand and a kid clinging to her leg. "You plan on joining us at some point?" The question, I learned, was rhetorical. Her voice was calm, but her eyes were wide with desperation. I'd mumble some excuse about making up time, but she wasn't impressed. She'd been with the kids all day, and she needed help.

So, a while back I instituted a new rule. No working after 5:00 p.m. At first, it was scary. What if there's an emergency and I had to work late? But I had to admit I was being a tad dramatic. I'm an editor and author, not a trauma surgeon. No one was going to die if I returned an email late or missed a typo. Very few people perish in editorial disasters. I did have deadlines, though. And I worried that staying out of my office in the evenings would hurt my productivity.

You must make peace with leaving things undone, with letting something slide, with being a good farmer who doesn't hurry because there's simply too much to do.

It has done the opposite. Setting a stop time for my work enabled me to focus better during the day. I knew I could no longer save work for later; there was no "overtime." To extend the sports metaphor, I had to leave it all on the field between 7:30 a.m. and 5:00 p.m.

It was a healthy acknowledgment of the limitations imposed by being a husband and father. Stepping away from my computer at 5:00 p.m. every day was a concrete way of confessing my finitude. I wasn't going to accomplish anything more for the day. It was over. The work would be there tomorrow. More editing. More writing. More emails.

My point isn't that you should adopt the same work schedule as me. But you should get comfortable with stopping, with embracing your finitude. Only God is infinite. You must make peace with leaving things undone, with letting something slide, with being a good farmer who doesn't hurry because there's simply too much to do.

"SYSTEMATIC NEGLECT"

Once you accept your limitations, then comes the hard part. Deciding what to drop. One leads naturally to the other. When I capped my workday at 5:00 p.m., I quickly realized there were some pet projects that had to go. For instance, I've been toying with the idea of trying to write a screenplay. I was considering coaching my son's basketball team. A friend asked if I would cohost a podcast. Those were all good things, but when I thought of cramming more into an already tight schedule, I knew the answer was no. Maybe I could do them later, but not now. Hollywood would have to wait for my brilliant screenplay. I simply didn't have time.

I had stumbled upon a principle that the organizational researcher Robert K. Greenleaf called "the art of systematic neglect." Greenleaf defined systematic neglect as the ability "to sort out the more important from the less important—and the important from the urgent—and attend to the more important, even though there may be penalties and censure for the neglect of something else."[7] I immediately fell in love with the term "systematic neglect," partially because it makes dropping tasks sound smart and sophisticated rather than lazy ("sorry I didn't take out the garbage, honey . . . systematic neglect"). But more than that, it just made sense. To show up for the most important things in your life, you must let other things go.

John Maxwell recounts the story of a young concert violinist who attributed her success to what she called "planned neglect." She explained, "When I was in music school, there were many things that demanded my time. When I went to my room after breakfast, I made my bed, straightened the room, dusted the floor, and did whatever else came to my attention. Then I hurried to my violin practice. I found I wasn't progressing as I thought I should, so I reversed things. Until my practice period was completed, I deliberately neglected everything else. That program of planned neglect, I believe, accounts for my success."[8]

I cringed as I read that story. I thought of how often I invert the order—enthusiastically tackling easy or trivial tasks while saving the most important ones for last . . . if I get to them at all. When I have a big project due, it's amazing how organized my bookshelf gets.

It's probably easy to see that there are more important things to do than straightening rooms and organizing bookshelves. Things get much trickier when you face a host of competing responsibilities that all seem crucial. It's why Greenleaf didn't recommend "random neglect." It must be systematic, strategic. And, as he acknowledged, there are always "penalties and censure" when you drop certain tasks from your schedule.

Around that time, I read the book *Essentialism: The Disciplined Pursuit of Less* by Greg McKeown. The book is about "discerning what is absolutely essential, then eliminating everything that is not, so we can make the highest possible contribution toward the things that really matter."[9] To McKeown, essentialism isn't just a productivity hack; it's a way of life. "Becoming an Essentialist means making cutting, condensing, and correcting a natural part of our daily routine—making editing a natural cadence in our lives."[10]

But how do you determine what to cut or condense?

Of course, there's the old tried-and-true Benjamin Franklin method of listing pros and cons—and seeing which list is longer. Greenleaf, who wrote for leaders, suggested they "constantly ask: 'How can I use myself to serve best?'" What a great question to guide your decisions! McKeown urges readers to apply what he calls the "90 Percent Rule."

"As you evaluate an option, think about the single most important criterion for that decision, and then simply give the option a score between 0 and 100. If you rate it any lower than 90 percent, then automatically change the rating to 0 and simply reject it."[11]

The 90 Percent Rule is a gut check, especially for people-pleasers like me. Can you think of commitments you've taken on that would fall below 90 percent? I can. Even once you set your sights on droppable activities, it can be tough to pull the trigger. But McKeown is adamant. "If it isn't a clear yes, then it's a clear no."[12]

There's a similar question I've started asking myself. I've found it tremendously clarifying.

If this opportunity or responsibility disappeared tomorrow, would my main feeling be sadness or relief? If the answer is relief, that's often a sign I need to drop it.

For a few years, I had a freelance sideline that paid well. At first, I enjoyed it. But after a while I struggled to maintain interest in the work. It just wasn't a great fit for my skills and passions. I was reluctant to walk away from it because the extra income was nice. But when I asked myself how I'd respond if it went away, I literally exhaled. It would be a huge relief, I realized. That was the answer I needed. I politely ended the gig and haven't regretted it for a second since.

Of course, we all have heavy responsibilities that we can't (and shouldn't) drop. I'm not talking about neglecting your family! But most of us have taken on optional activities that we should examine more carefully. Whatever method of discernment you employ, the important thing is that you're intentional about it. That you're not simply agreeing to things willy-nilly because you're too scared to say no.

THE ULTIMATE ESSENTIALIST

What you won't find in most literature on this topic, however, is the most important step of all. *Pray!* Here's a terrifying truth. You can scrutinize each opportunity and demand on your time and ask all the right questions—and still make the wrong decision. The problem is that your perspective, like everything else about you, is limited. You can't factor in every variable. You don't know the future. But God does. You need His guidance when it comes to how you spend the precious commodity of your time. I can think of times in my life when opportunities came up that seemed perfect on the surface. They checked every box and had more pros than cons. But after praying about them, I felt unsure, unsettled. I knew God was leading me in a different direction, so I passed them up. In each case, when I look back, it's clear I made the right decision.

Near the end of his book, McKeown points to the example of an unlikely essentialist: Jesus. He observes that "Jesus lives as a carpenter and then in his ministry lived without wealth, political position, or material belongings."[13] At first, I thought it was a stretch. After all, everyone wants to use Jesus to prove their point. But as I thought about it more, I became convinced he was right. And not just because Jesus lived a humble lifestyle. It was in the *way* He lived.

Jesus had a laser-like focus on His mission. Anyone who attempted to get Him to change the nature or timing of that mission earned a stiff rebuke (Matt. 16:23; John 7:6). Spending time with His Father was paramount, and He was willing to defy expectations to maintain that vital connection. That meant regularly slipping away from the crowds to pray, even though it caused His frustrated disciples to exclaim, "Everyone is looking for you!" But He didn't seem to mind. He only said and did what His Father called Him to say and do (John 5:19; 12:49), including going to the cross to die for the sins of the world. He resisted every temptation, distraction, and diversion designed to bump Him off course. When you read the Gospels, you can see how His entire life and ministry was aimed like an arrow on fulfilling His calling. He stripped away everything that threatened to jeopardize it.

Spending time with His Father was paramount, and He was willing to defy expectations to maintain that vital connection.

The older I get, the more I realize that following Him requires doing the same. As Jordan Raynor says, "If Jesus couldn't say yes to everything, neither can we."[14] At times, it will mean you won't be popular. You will not meet everyone's expectations. You will have to say no. You won't be able to do everything. You will have to let something slide. But ultimately, it will be worth it because it will enable you to fulfill the call God has placed on your life.

I'm writing these words from my home office. Every few minutes, I glance out my window. Each time I do, I see our lawn, blotchy and brown. It's ugly, but I've made peace with it. It's a reminder to let go of things that aren't important so I can give extra attention to the things that are. It reminds me that to show up for what's most important, you gotta let something slide.

REFLECT

Are you tempted to think you can "do it all"? Does facing your finitude feel confining or freeing?

Is there an opportunity you're currently considering? If it went away, would you feel sadness or relief?

Can you identify something you need to let slide? How would dropping nonessential tasks free you to focus on what matters most?

Chapter Eleven

Don't Be an Escape Artist

Stay Present by Nourishing Your Soul

Everyone got a little weird during the pandemic. I guess stress, uncertainty, isolation, and the ever-present threat of disease will do that to you.

I thought I was coping well, though I did indulge in a little retail therapy. I recall scrolling Amazon when I spotted a pair of sandals with hard plastic balls that dig into the soles of your feet. *That's a dumb idea,* I thought to myself. Then I read the description that claimed the tiny plastic balls stimulate different parts of your feet and bring healing to every area of your body. *Wow, that's even dumber*. Yet somehow a pair of size 12s found their way into my cart moments later. When they arrived at our doorstep, Grace opened the box and held them up like a dead bird. "What in the *world* are these?"

I tried them on, and gasped. Every step brought a fresh wave of pain. I couldn't tell if the other areas of my body felt any better. At least they didn't hurt as much as my feet.

In addition to making strange purchases, I began fantasizing about large, unattainable ones. I started spending an embarrassing amount of time on real estate sites like Zillow and Redfin. I've never been that materialistic, so the new habit took me by surprise. We didn't need a new house. Ours was fine. Nothing fancy, but it had enough bedrooms for our five-member family. It had a garage for all our junk. A nice, normal house. And I was relatively happy with it.

Until I started perusing other houses online. Our backyard is small, and I thought it would be nice to get a house where the kids had room to run around outside. But soon I realized our house was deficient in other ways as well. For instance, it had no theater room. I'd never really thought about having a theater in my house. But as I clicked through pictures of cavernous rooms with big screen TVs and surround sound, I suddenly wondered how I'd survived without one. How could I go on watching movies in the living room, like an animal? I also noticed that our house had no game room, no library, no home gym, no infrared sauna, and of course, no swimming pool.

I became more and more dissatisfied with our humble dwelling. When the kids ran through the living room as I tried to read, I'd think, *This is ridiculous, we need a recreation room for them to play in*. Each time we'd go in the backyard, I was annoyed. "This thing is the size of a postage stamp," I'd moan.

It was Grace who finally snapped me out of my stupor. One day she leaned over my shoulder as I gawked at houses hundreds of thousands of dollars beyond our budget. "What are you thinking?" she said. "We'll never have a house like that."

Not with that attitude, I thought.

But she was right. I was in a fantasy world. And that was the real problem. There was the creeping materialism, yes. The more concerning thing, however, is that I was engaging in escapist behavior. Every time I got bored with my work or annoyed by the kids, I'd whip out my phone, tap the Redfin app, and start scrolling. It was a little reprieve from the monotony and difficulty of everyday life. Yet instead of bringing relief, it was wasting time and draining my joy.

BENUMBED HEARTS

We've covered a range of strategies for showing up. We've talked about cracking open your Bible every day, showing up for church, being there for your family, and even showing up when you're suffering. It's impossible to overstate the importance of doing these things. But we need to discuss escapism too. Why? Because it holds us back from doing those vital things. Escapism is the tendency to engage in activities that prevent you from being present in your own life. For me, it was looking at nice houses online. For you, it might be playing *Call of Duty* till 3:00 a.m. every night. Or bingeing Netflix. Or scrolling Instagram. Or reading Wikipedia entries about the strangest ways people have died (oops, that's me again).

There are so many escape artists out there. I know a guy who spends countless hours arguing about politics in online chat rooms. He's unemployed and his wife finally left him after suffering years of mistreatment and neglect. But he knows exactly how the country should be run (just ask him!). I know another guy who's obsessed with end times theories. He spends a bizarre amount of time and energy conceiving of ever-more elaborate scenarios that might lead to the end of the world. I wonder how his considerable intelligence might be better used. I heard another guy lamenting that his wife spends so much time on Facebook, it's causing serious problems in their marriage. "She won't even put the phone down and look at me," he said. "I plead with her. 'Why are you spending all your time looking at other people's lives? I'm right here!'"

Some escapist behaviors are clearly sinful and destructive, like having an affair or doing drugs. But even the more acceptable forms of escapism can be dangerous. They may be fine activities in and of themselves. And it's great to have hobbies that fuel your passion and relieve stress. But when you find yourself spending an inordinate amount of time and energy on something, I think that's a clue you're indulging in escapist behavior. Whatever escape route you choose, the result is the same. It distracts you from being present in your life.

LIFE IS HARD

Why do we escape?

Well, at the risk of stating the obvious, life is hard. I'm on vacation right now. Relaxing, right? Not exactly. As those of us in the thick of parenting often remind each other, "vacationing is just parenting somewhere else." This morning we drove thirty minutes to see a waterfall. But the kids complained the whole way. "I'm sick of being stuck in the stupid car," one of them said. Then they started fighting with each other.

Finally, Grace had had enough. "That's it!" she announced. "Let's go back. This isn't even fun now." That's when I decided to remind her that the waterfall was *her* idea and none of us really wanted to go in the first place. You can imagine how that went over. By the time we got to the waterfall, the whole family was at each other's throats. And we proceeded to fight during the hike, pausing only to flash forced smiles for a family picture in front of the waterfall. Can't miss a good Instagram moment!

On the way home, we made up. The afternoon would be spent at the pool. Surely that would be fun and relaxing. And it was . . . for a while. Until Grace went down the waterslide and emerged clutching her left hand. Turns out she got her pinky finger caught in a crack on the way down, snapping it out of its socket. I frantically shuttled her and our wet children into the van, and back to our rented condo to change. Then it was off to urgent care. While the doctor wrenched Grace's finger back into place, I tried to keep the kids happy in the van. For three hours. When we finally returned to the condo, we were exhausted. And that's when we discovered that in our hurry to leave, we'd left the door wide open. The condo is in the forest and now I'm wondering if any woodland creatures made their way inside.

Escaping doesn't solve problems. If anything, it makes things worse.

Ah, vacations are so relaxing.

I don't mean to complain. I love my family like crazy. And I know I'm blessed to be able to take a vacation. But my point is that even activities that are supposed to be fun can be hard. More than once on this vacation, I've fought the urge to check out on my phone. I'm hardly unique. I talked to a fellow parent recently who confessed, "In the average day, there's not one thing that's just for me. I guess there's exercise, but I don't enjoy that. Maybe that's why I drink too much."

If the ordinary grind wears us down, just think what more trying circumstances can do. If you're reeling from the loss of a loved one. Or suffering from a chronic disease. Or dealing with unemployment. When challenges like this hit, the siren song of escapism can be overwhelming. Of course, escaping doesn't solve problems. If anything, it makes things worse. But it makes sense. Life is hard and it's tempting to escape.

THIRSTY CREATURES

I think there's an even more powerful force driving our escapism. It's simply this: We're thirsty. We yearn for connection. We long for wholeness. We dream of escaping our Groundhog Day existence and living a life of meaning and adventure. If those desires go unfulfilled, we turn to cheap replacements. We opt for synthetic transcendence. Think of the middle-aged woman starved for community who settles for watching people's lives on Instagram. Or the young man who drowns his frustrated attempts for love in online porn.

I'm not excusing any of these behaviors. But it's important to understand that they are often misguided attempts to fulfill core deep desires. Theologian Kelly M. Kapic, reflecting on the crazy amount of time the average American spends on screens, asks this: "What if rather than serving as the cause of our problems, the draw of mind-numbing screen time was a sign of a deeper malady? Maybe such escapism reveals a sickness in our souls that we have been neglecting."[1]

Indeed. Even my Redfin habit wasn't just about houses. When I'd daydream of buying a bigger place, I'd envision family and friends sitting around a huge table or streaming into a backyard spacious enough for a big party. I pictured us entertaining people. It was the middle of the pandemic, and I was longing for community. It's a little embarrassing to admit, but I think I was just lonely.

We get lonely for God too.

Tim Keller reflected on Freud's belief that religiosity was just repressed sexuality. "Close," wrote Keller. "Sexual desire is pent up religiosity. The need to be fulfilled."[2] I'm convinced that a lot of the dumb and dangerous habits we pick up are simply the result of failing to satisfy our spiritual longing. When there's a spiritual void, something else always rushes in to fill it.

In C. S. Lewis's book *The Screwtape Letters*, a demon named Screwtape advises a junior tempter on how to lead a new Christian away from God. Screwtape explains how his protégé need not use pleasures or "spectacular wickedness" to derail the Christian. Regular diversions, he assures his protégé, would do the trick: "You will find that anything or nothing is sufficient to attract his wandering attention. You will find him opening his arms to you and almost begging you to distract his purpose and benumb his heart."[3] But Screwtape explains that these distractions are effective only *after* the man has come to "increasingly dislike his religious duties" and has been tempted to "inattention in his prayers."[4]

When our connection with God weakens, we often turn to escapist behaviors. We "benumb" our hearts with silly distractions.

In other words, when our connection with God weakens, we often turn to escapist behaviors. We "benumb" our hearts with silly distractions. But our hearts weren't made to be satisfied by petty diversions. They can only be truly satisfied by God. Like Augustine famously put it, "Restless is the human heart until it comes to rest in You."[5]

DRY CISTERNS

All throughout the Old Testament we see the Israelites turning from God to worship idols. At one point, God delivers this stinging indictment through the mouth of His prophet Jeremiah: "[My people] have forsaken me, the spring of living water, and have dug their own cisterns, broken cisterns that cannot hold water" (Jer. 2:13).

There's deep sadness in those words. You can hear God's exasperation and pain at the betrayal. As the passage points out, though, the Israelites suffer the most. Only worshiping the one true God can quench their spiritual thirst. The cisterns of idolatry will only leave them parched.

We might shake our head at how often the ancient Israelites fell into idolatry, yet we aren't so different. Yeah, we probably don't literally bow before a stone deity, but whenever we turn to something else for the satisfaction that only God can provide, we're doing the same thing. We're digging our own cisterns. And like God warned, they cannot hold water.

If that sounds too abstract, let me get practical.

Your phone is a dry cistern. It can't quench the desire for connection and love that you crave.

Your work is a dry cistern if you've tied your sense of self-worth to it.

That 401(k) that you keep checking obsessively is a dry cistern. The security it promises is an illusion. The peace you seek can only be found in trusting God with your future.

The likes and comments on social media are dry cisterns. They'll never provide the approval that your soul craves.

Even your relationships with others can be dry cisterns when you heap expectations on them that only God can fulfill.

In the end it doesn't matter what cistern you choose. It will never hold water.

What can you do?

If you find yourself checking out, examine what's behind it. It may be that your life is hard and you're finding ways to check out. If that's the case, think through how you might swap out escapist behaviors for healthy ones. Instead of scrolling Twitter, go for a walk. Rather than playing video games, cook a meal. Instead of downing wine and watching Netflix, go out with friends. There are behaviors that refresh you and leave you better prepared to face the challenges in your life. I'm not saying things like Twitter and Netflix are never healthy. They can be when used in moderation. But many people use them to check out of real life. In general, escapism takes you out of the world; healthy habits drive you more deeply into it.

Most important, make sure you're turning to the right place to quench your spiritual thirst. Pray. Read Scripture. Gather with fellow believers. Get out in creation. Rest. These kinds of habits will help restore your soul and nurture that vital connection to your Creator. You don't have to escape. You don't need to reroute your deepest desires into meaningless activity. You don't have to keep licking dry cisterns. There is a source of living water that promises to quench the deepest thirst of your soul.

LIVING WATER

Take a quick trip with me. It's about six hundred years after the time of Jeremiah, and the Jews are celebrating the Feast of Booths. This was an annual feast that was basically a big weeklong camping trip. Jews from all over the empire would descend on Jerusalem and construct temporary dwellings ("booths") to commemorate their sojourn in the wilderness. But the feast was all about water. It was centered on giving thanks to God for the miraculous provision of water during their wandering in the desert.

On each day of the celebration, the high priest led a large procession to the Pool of Siloam. Using a large golden pitcher, he would draw water from the pool, and then lead the people back to the temple in Jerusalem. There, amid blasts from the shofar and singing of the people, the high priest would pour the water out on the altar as an offering to God. The water poured out hearkened back to God's provision for Israel, but it also looked ahead. It foreshadowed a day when all nations would join in the celebration honoring Israel's Messiah (Zech. 14:16–21).

But in one particular year, there was an interruption. On the last day of the celebration, perhaps at the very moment before the high priest was about to pour out the water, a young man from Nazareth stood up and shouted an audacious invitation.

"Let anyone who is thirsty come to me and drink. Whoever believes in me, as Scripture has said, rivers of living water will flow from within them" (John 7:37).

I love that scene. The young man was Jesus, of course. And His invitation probably wasn't welcomed by most. But for a moment, those present shifted their focus from the promise to the fulfillment, from a symbol of hope to its realization, from water that can quench physical thirst to the One who can satisfy spiritual longing.

Jesus still cries out. His invitation echoes down through the centuries, to every person with parched lips and a thirsty soul. If you find yourself tired of digging dry cisterns, it may be that you need to hear His invitation again.

"Come to me and drink."

Showing up for others is crucial. As we've seen, people need your presence. Your family, your church, your community. But without filling up on the water Jesus offers, you'll come to them dry and empty. You won't have much to offer. You'll resort to escapist behaviors that distract your mind and numb your soul.

So, take Jesus up on His invitation. Drop the dry cisterns, come to Him, and drink.

REFLECT

Do you ever find yourself engaging in behaviors to escape from your life? What circumstances or emotions cause you to want to check out?

How do you feel after engaging in escapist behaviors? What healthy activities could you choose instead?

Are there "dry cisterns" you use to try and quench your spiritual thirst? How would it change your life if you regularly accepted Christ's invitation to "come to me and drink"?

Chapter Twelve

Keep Wrestling with God

Don't Let Doubts Derail Your Faith

If you're a Christian for long enough, you'll notice that something sad starts to happen. A lot of the people who started the journey with you end up walking away.

They leave for various reasons and go out different doors. Some leave loudly, stating (or announcing online) that they no longer believe in God. Others drift away without so much as a whisper. There's no dramatic exit, but what's happened is just as clear and equally sad—they're gone.

I wrote my first book on the topic and interviewed twenty-somethings who shed their Christian identity. I won't wade into the thorny theological questions of what exactly happens in these situations. Can someone truly leave the faith? Were they ever Christians to begin with? I'm not sure. But I do know listening to their stories was humbling. Most, like me, had grown up in the church. They read the same Bible, sang the same songs, and prayed the same prayers. I finished that project with a sober awareness that their stories could easily be mine. I found myself repeating the words "there but for the grace of God go I."

They had a host of reasons for leaving. Many were hurt by other Christians. Some were drawn to behaviors that were incompatible with Christian beliefs. Others were plagued by doubt. The interesting thing to me is that some of the most faithful Christians I know have experienced identical challenges. They've been hurt by other Christians, dogged by temptations, or haunted by doubt. Sometimes all three. But they stayed. In some cases, these challenges actually drove them closer to God and deepened their faith.

Like the prophets, they didn't stop talking to God. Even when they were only half-convinced He was listening.

What was the difference between the ones who left and the ones who stayed? The only difference I could see is what they did with their trials. The first group ran away from God while the second ran toward Him. Instead of letting doubt and disappointment fester in darkness, they dragged it into the light. They brought it all to God. They hashed it out. They joined the great biblical tradition of prophets who expressed their grievances to God, often in harsh and accusatory language. But like the prophets, they didn't stop talking to God. Even when they were only half-convinced He was listening.

Counselors will tell you that the most dangerous thing in a marriage isn't when a couple is fighting. It's when they don't care enough to fight anymore. When the anger has hardened into silence. That's because indifference, not hate, is the opposite of love. Conflict is painful but it can be a sign of life.

I think that's also true in our relationship with God. Even if you're mad at God, there's hope. Your faith is still alive. You care enough to keep fighting. The danger comes when you go silent. When you let anger turn to apathy.

As we've seen, progress doesn't have to come through grand, heroic actions; small acts of faithfulness will do. I believe the same principle applies when we pass through a season of doubt or discouragement. Showing up in these hard times just means coming to God with your doubts and fears and frustrations. It doesn't require being dishonest about how you're feeling or denying the feeble state of your faith. It simply requires refusing to walk away.

HEALTHY MINDS AND SICK SOULS

In the landmark book *On the Varieties of Religious Experience*, nineteenth-century American psychologist William James described two different kinds of Christians. One he called the "healthy-minded" believer. These folks are natural optimists. They rarely if ever struggle with doubt. They're not drawn to the difficult questions about why there is evil and suffering in the world. James describes their souls as "sky-blue" and their "affinities are rather with flowers and birds . . . than with dark human passions . . . and they think no ill of man or God."

I know a lot of "healthy-minded" believers. They're not simpletons. They just see the sunnier side of life. They take God's promises at face value and walk out their faith unencumbered by doubt.

I envy them, probably because I fall into James's second category, what he calls the "sick soul." For this type of believer, faith doesn't come easily. They're besieged by doubts. They grapple with hard questions. As William James writes, they "cannot so swiftly throw off the burden of the consciousness of evil, but are congenitally fated to suffer from its presence." Even their joy is tempered by shadows. "From the bottom of every fountain of pleasure . . . something bitter rises up: a touch of nausea, a falling dead of the delight, a whiff of melancholy."[1]

James named figures such as the reformer Martin Luther and novelist Leo Tolstoy as examples of sick souls. And, as you might guess from his vivid descriptions of this temperament, James placed himself in the category too. If you see yourself in James's description of the sick soul, welcome to the party. A party where there's a lot of anxiety, second-guessing, and bouts of existential dread.

I should add, though, that for James, the label was not a pejorative. The sick soul's path isn't easy, but that doesn't mean they're unfaithful. As one commenter summarized, "James described this type of believer as one who grapples with the evils of life and takes on religion even if it causes distress. The sick soul doubts, is frustrated, struggles with God and faith, and yet sticks with it."[2]

I'm convinced a lot of the authors of Scripture match James's definition of a sick soul. Who can read Paul's anguished accounts of battling sin without hearing the cry of a sick soul? "What a wretched man I am! Who will rescue me from this body that is subject to death?" (Rom. 7:24). Or consider David, who frequently railed against the unfairness of life and aired his feelings of abandonment. "How long, LORD? Will you forget me forever?" (Ps. 13:1). Then there's Solomon. The entire book of Ecclesiastes reads like a sick-soul manifesto. "It is better to go to a house of mourning than to go to a house of feasting, for death is the destiny of everyone" (Eccl. 7:2). Yikes.

These biblical writers went toe-to-toe with the reality of evil and suffering. They asked hard questions. They were honest about pain and injustice. They even accused God of being silent or indifferent to their plight. But again, here's the key. They didn't give up on God. They saw the darkness but placed their trust in the only One who could ultimately dispel it. Even when they didn't understand what was going on, they kept coming back to God, if only to complain. They had stubborn faith, the kind that allowed the famous sufferer Job to say of God, "Though he slay me, yet will I hope in him" (Job 13:15).

They didn't give up on God. They saw the darkness but placed their trust in the only One who could ultimately dispel it.

Doubt is inescapable. My friend Dominic Done says that "in our time, we all breathe the secondhand smoke of doubt." That reality is amplified for those of us with a sick-soul disposition. Yet it doesn't have to destroy our faith. Those biblical writers provide a template for those of us who find ourselves assailed by doubt and despair. We follow their example by continuing to pray and struggle and hope. Even when we feel ourselves drawn to the darker side of life, we keep searching for the light. We remember that "the sick soul doubts, is frustrated, struggles with God and faith, and yet sticks with it."

THE FIGHTER

There's one person in the Bible who *literally* wrestled with God: Jacob.

If you've read the book of Genesis, you're familiar with Jacob's antics. He famously conned his older brother, Esau, out of his birthright, bribing his brother with a bowl of soup. Later, he dressed up in animal furs to fool his dying father into giving him the blessing, and it worked. Then he fled his childhood home before Esau could kill him.

After years on the lam, Jacob receives a scary message. Esau "is coming to meet you, and four hundred men are with him" (Gen. 32:6). Jacob is "greatly afraid and distressed" by the news (v. 7 NKJV). Jacob, ever the schemer, shifts into survival mode. He sends herds of animals ahead of him as a gift to Esau, hoping to assuage his brother's wrath. Then he divides his servants and livestock into two camps. That way, if his brother attacks one camp, the other one can escape. Finally, he sends his family away.

The night before meeting Esau, Jacob is all alone. That's when the divine wrestling match happens. A stranger appears. Initially, we're told nothing of the man's identity, just that a fight ensues. They wrestle all night. Jacob realizes there's something special about the stranger because he begs the man to bless him. The man tries to break away and leave, but Jacob clings to him, even after he dislocates Jacob's hip. "I will not let you go unless you bless me" (Gen. 32:26).

Then the man does something odd. He renames Jacob. "Your name will no longer be Jacob, but Israel, because you have struggled with God and with humans and have overcome" (v. 28). Then he grants Jacob's request and blesses him. Jacob limps toward the sunrise a different man. The dreaded encounter with Esau turns out to be a reunion. The brothers embrace and weep.

It's one of the strangest stories in all of Scripture, which is really saying something. Is the man Jacob wrestles with an angel? God in human form? Jacob seems to think so, exclaiming with wonder, "I saw God face to face, and yet my life was spared" (Gen. 32:30).

He knew the only thing more dangerous than wrestling with God is letting God go.

I've always been drawn to the story. Perhaps that's strange, too, because Jacob isn't exactly a sympathetic character. He's a scoundrel. As author Frederick Buechner writes, "Jacob was never satisfied. He wanted the moon, and if he'd ever managed to bilk heaven out of that, he would have been back the next morning for the stars to go with it."[3] Instead of this being a story about a hero with sterling character, it plays out the way so many Bible stories do: with God extending grace to someone who clearly doesn't deserve it.

Jacob was far from perfect, but he got one thing right. He hung on to God. He was flawed, but he had faith. And tenacity. He knew the only thing more dangerous than wrestling with God is letting God go.

THE MAKE-OR-BREAK ASSUMPTION

Parenting gives you a crash course in theology. Think about it. You have someone made in your image. You love this person so desperately you can hardly stand it. Yet half the time they're convinced you're trying to make them miserable when everything you're doing is actually for their ultimate good!

My youngest once threw a massive fit because I demanded she hold my hand in a busy parking lot. Of course, she was completely oblivious to the fact that her desire to run amid moving vehicles could put her life in danger. From her perspective, I was just a monster ruining her fun by imposing arbitrary restrictions. Finally, I had to pick her up and hold her tightly against my chest as she thrashed about trying to break free.

Such moments help me see things from God's perspective. Our doubts don't usually arise in a vacuum. They tend to come during seasons of suffering. And when we suffer, it's easy to assume God is indifferent or inflicting pain arbitrarily. Like a strong-willed toddler, we thrash about failing to see the bigger picture. We can't imagine how what God is doing could be what's best for us.

The timing of Jacob's wrestling match with God was no coincidence. It happened on the hardest night of his life, when he was scared to death that he was going to die. When he's sitting in the dark all alone.

We're not so different from Jacob. We tend to do our best tussling with God in the dark, in those moments when we're fearful or overwhelmed. We can feel a little sheepish turning to God in such moments. Especially if we've been ignoring Him during the good times. I know I've started a lot of prayers by saying, "God, I'm sorry I'm only coming to you now . . . when I'm in trouble." If Jacob could wrestle with God when he hit rock bottom, we can too.

And in fact, that's the best possible thing you can do in such circumstances. Because in coming to God, even if we're uncertain or angry, it still shows that we trust Him, that we haven't given up.

I've noticed another thing as my children grow. They trust me more. Don't get me wrong. They still argue and complain. But they no longer assume I'm a sadistic monster bent on destroying their lives. Why? Because they know I love them. They're starting to understand that, even when they can't comprehend my actions, I still have their best interest in mind.

That's a good theology lesson too. If we have a bedrock trust in God's goodness, we don't need to know everything. We don't need to solve every theological riddle. We can keep walking through the storm, confident that we're led by a good God.

My friend Kevin Miller is an Anglican priest, a brilliant writer, and one of the most faithful men I know. Perhaps that's why I was surprised when he admitted going through a time of intense doubting. These weren't doubts he'd weathered as a young man; he was in his fifties at the time. What helped him through? He realized that though several core beliefs had come under fire in his mind, he still believed that God was good. And because of that, he knew his faith could endure. He called the question of God's goodness "the make-or-break assumption." If God is good, he reasoned, that meant he could trust Him, even in the face of uncertainty.

STUMBLING AFTER JESUS

At the beginning of this chapter, I talked about seeing people leave the faith. That's a gut-wrenching experience, especially if the people in question are family members or friends. But what I've found even more disorienting has been watching Christian leaders fall.

A few years ago, one of my former pastors was arrested in a sex trafficking sting. I read the news story about the arrest in disbelief. My mind drifted back to the many powerful sermons I heard him preach. How could someone with such a deep grasp of Scripture do something so despicable?

It was a question I asked again when I read that my favorite Christian apologist, Ravi Zacharias, had been accused of sexually inappropriate behavior. Initially I hoped the allegations were false, but after his own ministry concluded a four-month investigation, the ugly truth spilled out. The famous Christian intellectual had leveraged his position of power to abuse massage therapists in the US and overseas for more than a decade. I was stunned.

When I read his books as a young man, I was electrified. He combined a vigorous intellectual defense of the faith with a winsomeness that moved thousands closer to Christ, including me. I couldn't reconcile his ministry with the man revealed by the report. How could he abuse hundreds of vulnerable image bearers—and then lie to everyone for years to cover it up? I had no answers.

We can pretend that we're not affected by such stories, but we are. They shake us. It's confusing to see someone you once looked to for spiritual guidance fall so dramatically.

It's awful to see leaders that you respected fall, but I've learned from it. I've learned never to put my hope in anyone other than Jesus. People will always let you down. The earlier you learn that lesson, the better. The Bible says to fix our eyes on Jesus, "the author and finisher of our faith" (Heb. 12:2 NKJV). To fix your eyes on anyone else, no matter how godly or charismatic, only leads to disappointment.

Such stories also remind me that true success in the Christian life isn't about being talented or famous or having a huge impact. It's about faithfulness. That doesn't mean you don't have struggles. It just means you stay the course even when you do.

The Christian life is a marathon where you win just by finishing. Where you keep stumbling after Jesus when all your heroes are gone. Where you grab hold of God and refuse to let go.

REFLECT

How does it affect you to see people walking away from the faith? What about when you see Christian leaders fall?

Do you see yourself as more of what William James calls a "healthy-minded believer" or a "sick soul"? What are the advantages and drawbacks of each kind of disposition?

In what ways have you wrestled with God? Has it strengthened your faith?

Epilogue

Showing Up Is Just the Beginning

Writing this book was a slog.

Every time I sat down to write, other activities clamored for my attention. I'd think, *Maybe I should check my email (it's been almost five minutes). Or I need to clean the van. Or scoop the cat's litter. Or schedule a colonoscopy.* Anything was better than facing the blank page.

Even once I forced myself to write, the words seemed to get stuck in my brain. I remember returning from the coffee shop one afternoon discouraged. A three-hour stint had yielded only a few hundred words—and I didn't like any of them. When I shared my frustration with Grace, she turned my advice around on me.

"Just show up."

That's the key, of course. One writing session wasn't very productive. But a commitment to apply my pants to a seat in front of a computer every day produced results. The stuck words began to trickle and, occasionally, flow. Eventually they became a book.

What's true in writing is true in life. Just showing up is powerful.

That might seem too simple. I can already hear the objections.

Don't we need to do more than just show up? Doesn't that set the bar too low? Should we be content with a mediocre Christian life where we aim to do the bare minimum?

If that's your impression, let me reassure you. That's not what I'm saying. Showing up is the starting point, not the end goal. It's the vehicle, not the destination. It can feel silly to start small. Showing up doesn't feel like enough. But it makes the daunting doable. It enables you to overcome the inertia of inaction. It helps you get unstuck.

What's even more exciting is that God rewards small acts of faithfulness. He delights in multiplying our meager efforts to accomplish what we could never do on our own. Just think of all the stories in Scripture where people showed up and saw God do amazing things.

Moses shows up at Pharoah's palace. But God does the miracles.

David shows up to fight Goliath. But it's the Lord who delivers the giant into his hands.

Elijah shows up for the showdown at Mount Carmel. Then God sends fire from heaven.

A little boy shares his lunch of loaves and fishes. Jesus feeds the multitudes.

The servants fill the jars with water. Jesus turns it to wine.

You serve the same God. Like those characters, the outcome of your battles doesn't depend on your strength alone. That's good news. The giants you face are too big for you anyway. So just show up and leave the rest to God.

Acknowledgments

I want to start by thanking the little people. That's right, my children. Without your constant noise and interruptions as I tried to write in my highly accessible home office, this book would have been done much sooner. But you also gave me a lot of material to work with, so let's call it even. Seriously, you're great kids and I'm so proud of you. Showing up for you is a delight.

This book would have never materialized without the insights and encouragement of my wonderful wife, Grace. You live out the message of this book every day and everyone around you is richer for it. I also think you're very pretty. What are you doing this Friday?

I also want to thank Grace's parents, Brian and Jane. Not only did you let me marry your daughter, but you listened to early material from this book and gave helpful feedback. Jane, I've benefited greatly from your spiritual insights. Brian, I may have won all the theological debates we've had but you've taught me a thing or two along the way.

Thanks to my parents, Art and Margee, for raising a man so spiritual and handsome. And humble. OK, for real, I don't even know where to start. Mom, you gave me my love for the written word. And dad, you were the best father a guy could hope for. And you're still helping me. Thanks for letting me use your story in this book. Your lifetime of faithfulness and ministry continues to bear fruit.

Thanks to all my friends who continue reading my stuff, even though they have an inside view of what a strange goofball I am. Friends like Marshall Allen, Jason Plunkett, Jody Jasurda, Kyle Rohane, Paul Pastor, Dan Darling, and Kevin Miller. Same goes for my brothers David, Darren, and Danny. Thanks for letting me sleep in your rooms when we were growing up because I was scared of aliens. Even when I was thirteen and the whole thing was getting kind of ridiculous.

Thanks to all my friends on Twitter, especially the guy who runs a Drew Dyck parody account. You obviously have too much time on your hands, but I'm proud you chose to waste it on me. People say Twitter is a dumpster fire (and it is) but I've made a lot of wise and gracious friends there too.

Writing is a solo enterprise, but publishing a book is a collaborative effort. This book wouldn't have happened without Randall Payleitner taking the risk on publishing yet another book from an obscure Canadian. I'm indebted to Connor Sterchi, whose careful and patient editing made the manuscript much better. I'm also grateful for my colleagues at Moody—Trillia Newbell, John Hinkley, Judy Dunagan, Kevin Mungons, and Catherine Parks. You're truly the best team in the business. Thanks for putting up with me.

Last, I want to thank God. Sounds grandiose, I know, but I'm crazy enough to think we have a relationship. The only reason we do, of course, is because He showed up for me—and for all of us—in the person of His Son, Jesus. For that, I'll be eternally grateful.

Notes

CHAPTER 1: JOIN THE PLODDERS

1. *Cambridge Dictionary*, s.v. "plodding," https://dictionary.cambridge.org/us/dictionary/english/plodding.
2. The Free Dictionary, s.v. "plod along," https://idioms.thefreedictionary.com/plod.
3. George Smith, *The Life of William Carey: Shoemaker and Missionary* (Minneapolis: J. M. Dent, 1922), vii.
4. James Clear, *Atomic Habits: An Easy & Proven Way to Build Good Habits & Break Bad Ones* (New York: Penguin, 2018), 195.
5. Luke Simmons, Twitter post, January 17, 2023, 4:05 p.m., https://twitter.com/lukedsimmons/status/1615500549427957761?s=20&t=zSAJo3kKGz5M3UBSQl5wlQ.
6. Daniel Darling, *The Characters of Creation* (Chicago: Moody Publishers, 2022), 141.
7. Frank Deaville Walker, *William Carey: Missionary, Pioneer, and Statesman* (Chicago: Moody Publishers, 1951), 285.
8. "Art: Fantastic Catalan," *TIME*, January 28, 1952, https://content.time.com/time/subscriber/article/0,33009,806302,00.html.
9. Rainer Zerbst, *Gaudí: A Life Devoted to Architecture* (Cologne: Taschen, 1997), 192.
10. Jordan Raynor, *Master of One: Find and Focus on the Work You Were Created to Do* (Colorado Springs: Waterbrook, 2021), 26.

CHAPTER 2: SHOW UP IN PERSON

1. Kaia Hubbard, "Outside of Sleeping, Americans Spend Most of Their Time Watching Television," US News & World Report, July 22, 2021, usnews.com/news/best-states/articles/2021-07-22/americans-spent-more-time-watching-television-during-covid-19-than-working.
2. Dan Avery, "Americans Spent a Third of Waking Hours on Mobile Devices in 2021, Report Finds," CNET, January 12, 2022, https://www.cnet.com/tech/services-and-software/americans-spent-a-third-of-waking-hours-on-mobile-devices-in-2021-report-finds/.
3. Theresa Gaffney, "Rates of Depression and Anxiety Climbed Across the Globe in 2020, Analysis Finds," *Stat News*, October 8, 2021, https://www.statnews.com/2021/10/08/mental-health-covid19-pandemic-global/.
4. Darryl L. Forbes, Twitter post, November 20, 2022, 6:22 p.m., https://twitter.com/darrylforbes_/status/1594516563079618560?s=20.
5. Adam Grant, Twitter post, November 29, 2022, 11:46 a.m., https://twitter.com/AdamMGrant/status/1597678377741488128?s=20&t=QnHhraaE3HCp6_GGqjmR8g.
6. Philip Yancey, *Where Is God When It Hurts?* (Grand Rapids: Zondervan, 1977), 182.

CHAPTER 3: FIND GOD'S WILL WITH YOUR FEET

1. NKJV.
2. A. W. Tozer, "Four Ways to Find God's Will," *Moody Monthly*, June 1970, 79.
3. Kevin DeYoung, *Just Do Something: A Liberating Approach to Finding God's Will* (Chicago: Moody Publishers, 2009), 59.
4. Dominic Done, Twitter post, December, 1, 2021, 4:54 p.m., https://twitter.com/DominicDone/status/1466209104326656000?s=20&t=UbLrIlSdO-NvXg7gKOl0-g.

CHAPTER 4: BE A "LONG-HAUL HERO"

1. Pete Davis, *Dedicated: The Case for Commitment in an Age of Infinite Browsing* (New York: Avid Reader Press, 2021), 3.

2. Ibid.
3. Ibid., 5.
4. Ibid., 6.
5. H.B. Charles Jr., Daniel Darling, Lee Eclov et al., "Who Is Your Greatest Pastoral Influence?," *Christianity Today*, October 2016, https://www.christianitytoday.com/pastors/2016/october-web-exclusives/who-is-greatest-pastoral-influence.html.
6. Ibid.
7. Donald Keys, *Earth at Omega: Passage to Planetization* (Brookline, MA: Branden, 1985), 79.
8. Gaetano Baluffi and Denis Gargan, *The Charity of the Church: A Proof of Her Divinity* (Dublin: M. H. Gill and Son, 1885), 16.
9. Glenn Packiam, Instagram post, June 17, 2021, https://www.instagram.com/p/CQRJa09nK79/?igshid=YmMyMTA2M2Y%3D.
10. C. S. Lewis, *The Collected Letters of C. S. Lewis: Volume II*, ed. Walter Hooper (New York: HarperCollins, 2004), Letter of Dec. 20, 1946.

CHAPTER 5: PLAY THE ROLE

1. Heather Thompson Day and Seth Day, *I'll See You Tomorrow: Building Relational Resilience When You Want to Quit* (Nashville: Nelson, 2022), 2.
2. Ibid.
3. Ibid.

CHAPTER 6: JUST CRACK OPEN YOUR BIBLE

1. "Lifeway Research: Americans Are Fond of the Bible, Don't Actually Read It," Lifeway Research, April 25, 2017, https://research.lifeway.com/2017/04/25/lifeway-research-americans-are-fond-of-the-bible-dont-actually-read-it/; "Frequency of Reading the Bible Among Adults in the United States from 2018 to 2021," Statista, May 2021, https://www.statista.com/statistics/299433/bible-readership-in-the-usa/.
2. Josh Howerton, Twitter post, December 1, 2018, 4:04 p.m., https://twitter.com/howertonjosh/status/1069019471942172672?s=20.
3. Tish Harrison Warren, *Liturgy of the Ordinary* (Downers Grove, IL: IVP, 2016), 35.

4. Eugene Peterson, *A Long Obedience in the Same Direction* (Downers Grove, IL: IVP, 1980), 54.
5. Ibid., 48.
6. Trillia Newbell, *52 Weeks in the Word: A Companion for Reading through the Bible in a Year* (Chicago: Moody Publishers, 2022).
7. "The Power of Habit: Q&A with Author Charles Duhigg," Penguin Random House Library Marketing, November 9, 2011, https://penguinrandomhouselibrary.com/2011/11/09/power-of-habit-qa-with-author-charles-duhigg/.
8. For some simple tasks 30 days is enough to establish a habit. For other, more complex behaviors, it may take up to 66 days.
9. James Clear, *Atomic Habits: An Easy and Proven Way to Build Good Habits and Break Bad Ones* (New York: Penguin Random House, 2018), 163.
10. Drake Baer, "The Secret to Changing Your Habits: Start Incredibly Small," *Fast Company*, December 5, 2013, https://www.fastcompany.com/3022830/the-secret-to-changing-your-habits-start-incredibly-small.
11. BJ Fogg, *Tiny Habits: The Small Changes That Change Everything* (New York: Harvest, 2021), 28.
12. William Johnston, "Monasticism," Britannica.com, https://www.britannica.com/topic/monasticism/Cenobitic#ref422760.
13. Nick Needham, *The Early Church Fathers: Daily Readings* (Fearn, Scotland: Christian Focus Publications, 2017), loc. 2306, Kindle.

CHAPTER 7: SHOW UP FOR CHURCH

1. Wendy Wang, "The Decline of Church in COVID America," *Institute for Family Studies*, January 20, 2022, https://ifstudies.org/blog/the-decline-in-church-attendance-in-covid-america.
2. Drew Dyck, Twitter post, April 27, 2022, 5:15 p.m., https://twitter.com/drewdyck/status/1519470335954878464?s=20&t=qoQz9FQlRwlEtPT3OMq8Xw.
3. Dave Gipson, "Go to Church," October 23, 2021, https://davegipson.net/go-to-church/.

4. John E. Rotelle, ed., *The Works of Saint Augustine: Vol. 1., Sermons on the Old Testament* (New York: New City Press, 1990), 302.
5. Walker Hayes and Craig Allen Cooper, *Glad You're Here: Two Unlikely Friends Breaking Bread and Fences* (Chicago: Moody Publishers, 2022), 22.
6. Ibid., 23.
7. Ibid.
8. Ibid., 23–24.
9. Josh Howerton, Twitter thread, February 23, 2022, https://twitter.com/howertonjosh/status/1496602690624704513?lang=en.
10. Tyler J. Vanderweele and Brendan Case, "Empty Pews Are an American Public Health Crisis," October 19, 2021, *Christianity Today*, https://www.christianitytoday.com/ct/2021/november/church-empty-pews-are-american-public-health-crisis.html.
11. *The Simpsons*, season 12, episode 1.
12. Matt Smethurst, "The Church Irreplaceable," Desiring God, July 19, 2020, https://www.desiringgod.org/articles/the-church-irreplaceable.
13. Ibid.
14. Collin Hansen and Jonathan Leeman, *Rediscover Church: Why the Body of Christ Is Essential* (Wheaton: Crossway, 2021), 147.
15. Dean Inserra, Twitter post, April 15, 2023, 5:35 p.m., https://twitter.com/deaninserra/status/1647398245763624961?s=20.
16. Darren Whitehead, Instagram video, August 15, 2022, https://www.instagram.com/reel/ChS8PK9jj2g/?igshid=MDJmNzVkMjY%3D.

CHAPTER 8: LEARN TO WALK IN THE RAIN

1. Portions of this chapter are adapted from "You Can Break Your Brain: And 4 Other Things I've Learned from My Struggle with Anxiety and Depression," DrewDyck.com, July 12, 2018, https://www.drewdyck.com/post/you-can-break-your-brain-and-4-other-things-i-ve-learned-from-my-struggle-with-depression-anxiety.
2. Timothy Keller, *Walking with God through Pain and Suffering* (New York: Dutton, 2013), 3.

3. Vicks NyQuil TV Spot, "Dave," September 15, 2014, https://www.ispot.tv/ad/7ClP/vicks-nyquil-dave.
4. Lizzy Acker, "Do Oregonians Really Hate Umbrellas?," *The Oregonian*, March 13, 2017, https://www.oregonlive.com/trending/2017/03/do_oregonians_really_hate_umbr.html.
5. Bethany, her family, and her medical team were unsure she would survive her original COVID infection in 2020. But she did—and as of December 2022 has had it five times since! Her painful long-haul recovery connected her with other specialists who were able to identify additional underlying issues: Hypokalemic Periodic Paralysis (an ultra-rare, genetic neuromuscular disease), POTS, and Mast Cell Activation Syndrome (MCAS).
6. Scott Sauls quoting Elisabeth Kübler-Ross in *Beautiful People Don't Just Happen* (Grand Rapids: Zondervan, 2022), 19.

CHAPTER 9: PRACTICE INCARNATION

1. *This American Life*, episode 539, "The Leap," November 7, 2014, https://www.thisamericanlife.org/539/transcript.
2. Ibid.
3. Ibid.
4. Ibid.
5. Ibid.
6. Ibid.
7. Ibid.
8. Ibid.
9. Ibid.
10. Marshall Allen, "What We Do Matters More Than What We Say," Marshall Allen Substack, March 15, 2022, https://marshallallen.substack.com/p/what-we-do-matters-more-than-what.
11. Christine Fain, Twitter post, June 17, 2019, 1:25 p.m., https://twitter.com/cfain63/status/1140717170516811777?s=20&t=p_7FRLhtCY-RMVajGb7OMA.
12. Daniel J. Siegel and Tina Payne Bryson, *The Power of Showing Up* (New York: Ballantine, 2020) 22, 23.

13. Drew Dyck, Twitter post, March 5, 2022, 9:57 a.m., https://twitter.com/drewdyck/status/1500168667111124994.
14. Kara Powell, "Preventing Teenage 'Faith Drift,'" Karapowell.com, August 13, 2018, https://karapowell.com/2018/08/preventing-teenage-faith-drift/.

CHAPTER 10: LET SOMETHING SLIDE

1. 4k Weeks Poster, https://4kweeks.com/products/poster.
2. Oliver Burkeman, *Four Thousand Weeks: Time Management for Mortals* (New York: Farrar, Straus and Giroux, 2021), 3.
3. Ibid.
4. Kelly M. Kapic, *You're Only Human: How Your Limits Reflect God's Design and Why That's Good News* (Grand Rapids: Brazos Press, 2022), 15.
5. Adam Grant, Twitter post, October 25, 2022, 9:02 a.m., https://twitter.com/AdamMGrant/status/1584938446870573057?s=20&t=5D7sUxfqFy6rwna188EMUw.
6. Reinhold Niebuhr, *The Irony of American History* (Chicago: Charles Scribner and Sons, 1952), 63.
7. Robert K. Greenleaf, *The Servant as Leader* (Indianapolis: Greenleaf Center for Servant Leadership, 1970, 1991), 8.
8. John Maxwell, *Developing the Leader Within You* (Nashville: Thomas Nelson, 1993), 28–29.
9. *Essentialism* book description, https://www.amazon.com/Essentialism-Disciplined-Pursuit-Greg-McKeown/dp/0804137382.
10. Greg McKeown, *Essentialism: The Disciplined Pursuit of Less* (New York: Crown Publishing Group, 2014), 163.
11. Ibid., 104.
12. Ibid., 109.
13. Ibid., 227.
14. Jordan Raynor, *Master of One: Find and Focus on the Work You Were Created to Do* (Colorado Springs: Waterbrook, 2020), 124.

CHAPTER 11: DON'T BE AN ESCAPE ARTIST

1. Kelly M. Kapic, *You're Only Human: How Your Limits Reflect God's Design and Why That's Good News* (Grand Rapids: Brazos Press, 2022), 10.

2. Tim Keller, Twitter post, February 26, 2019, 11:23 a.m., https://twitter.com/timkellernyc/status/1100476344905932801?s=20&t=Fx4NWPsrFsgtZ_k5gogyUw.
3. C. S. Lewis, *The Screwtape Letters* (London: Geoffrey Bles, 1942), 59.
4. Ibid.
5. Augustine, *Confessions* (Alachua, FL: Bridge-Logos, 2003), 11.

CHAPTER 12: KEEP WRESTLING WITH GOD

1. William James, *The Varieties of Religious Experience* (Cambridge, MA: Harvard University Press, 1985), 73.
2. "William James and the Sick Soul," History of Theories in Psychology, Abilene Christian University, March 21, 2011, https://blogs.acu.edu/1120_PSYC49301/2011/03/21/william-james-and-the-sick-soul/.
3. Frederick Buechner, *Peculiar Treasures: A Biblical Who's Who* (New York: Harper & Row, 1979), 57.

"Few books have the potential to change your life as much as this one."

—Lee Strobel

Your Future Self Will Thank You is a compassionate and humorous guide to reclaiming your willpower. It shares proven, practical strategies for success, as well as biblical principles that will help you whether you want to lose a few pounds, conquer addiction, or kick your nail-biting habit.

978-0-8024-1829-6 | also available as eBook

Is joy the icing on the cake of life—
or the fuel on which it runs?

Joy is possible. The authors show how to build habits that fill our lives with joy and satisfaction. Based on the latest neuroscience and attachment theory—but written in everyday language—this book is easy to comprehend. The authors provide exercises and tools you can put into practice immediately.

978-0-8024-3139-4 | also available as eBook

Hyper-spiritual approaches to finding God's will don't work. It's time to try something new:

Give up.

God doesn't need to tell us what to do at each fork in the road. **He already revealed His plan for our lives: love Him with our whole hearts, obey His Word, and after that, do what we like.** No reason to be directionally challenged. Just do something.

978-0-8024-1159-4 | also available as eBook and audiobook